MAJOR RELIGIONS OF INDIA

New insights into Hinduism,
Jainism, Buddhism and Sikhism

MAJOR RELIGIONS OF INDIA

SUSUNAGA WEERAPERUMA

Edited by
SUDHAKAR S. DIKSHIT

MOTILAL BANARSIDASS PUBLISHERS
PRIVATE LIMITED • DELHI

First Edition: Bombay, 1985
Reprint: Delhi, 1996

ISBN: 81-208-1425-8

Also available at:

MOTILAL BANARSIDASS
41 U.A. Bungalow Road, Jawahar Nagar, Delhi 110 007
8 Mahalaxmi Chamber, Warden Road, Mumbai 400 026
120 Royapettah High Road, Mylapore, Madras 600 004
Sanas Plaza, Subhash Nagar, Pune 411 002
16 St. Mark's Road, Bangalore 560 001
8 Camac Street, Calcutta 700 017
Ashok Rajpath, Patna 800 004
Chowk, Varanasi 221 001

PRINTED IN INDIA

BY JAINENDRA PRAKASH JAIN AT SHRI JAINENDRA PRESS,
A-45 NARAINA, PHASE I, NEW DELHI 110 028
AND PUBLISHED BY NARENDRA PRAKASH JAIN FOR
MOTILAL BANARSIDASS PUBLISHERS PRIVATE LIMITED,
BUNGALOW ROAD, DELHI 110 007

INTRODUCTION

Every aspect of Indian life and culture has been influenced by religion either directly or indirectly and religious ideas have permeated Indian philosophy, literature, music, art and architecture. They have profoundly conditioned the outlook on life of the Indian people. Those wishing to understand the mysterious complexity that is India must first of all study her religions. Furthermore, no one interested in the history of civilization should ignore the impact of Indian religious thought on human consciousness in many different countries.

The scope of this book is confined to the examination of those major religious movements that originated in the subcontinent of India — Hinduism, Jainism, Buddhism and Sikhism. It does not include relgions that were born elsewhere, such as Islam, Zoroastrianism, Judaism and Christianity, although there are millions of Indians who belong to these faiths.

The book is primarily concerned with the human implications of certain religious concepts, beliefs and practices. After elucidating some of the basic ideas and beliefs of each religion, I have proceeded to discuss their psychological significance today. It is far more important to understand the social and psychological reasons why people become attached to certain doctrines than merely to be conversant with the doctrines themselves. If the cherished consolations and satisfactions that human beings derive from their particular creeds are uncovered by probing into them, then such investigations into Indian religions can become immensely valuable.

The four major religions of India dealt with in this book are the product of a people with a common historical and cultural heritage and hence they have many common features. Still the ideological differences that separate them should never be overlooked. There is a widespread notion in Western countries that all Indians subscribe to one general theory of Karma, whereas the truth is that each Indian religion has its own different theory of Karma. I have considered each major religion in a separate chapter instead of following the alternative course of considering specific subjects, such as God or reincarnation, and then treating religious ideas as mere secondary aspects of those topics. Each religion is an organic whole and to view it as being otherwise will only do violence to its essential character.

Religion should heighten the intelligence of man instead of reducing it to servility, where he is prepared to accept any dogma with an attitude of unquestioning acquiescence. Is a mind given to blind believing a religious mind? Surely only the mind intent on critical investigation deserves to be looked upon as being truly religious. What is the use of religion, if it does not elevate the mind, so that it becomes a fine instrument that is highly sceptical, alert and ever-watchful? The illumined mind, constantly awake, naturally becomes a light to the world. Let us hearken to the words of the Buddha:

> "Watchfulness is the road of immortality: unwatchfulness is the road of death. The watchful ones never die: those who fail to watch are already as dead."

Susunaga Weeraperuma

ACKNOWLEDGEMENTS

There are several reasons why I am particularly thankful to Mr. Sudhakar S. Dikshit, the founder and Editor of Chetana. When I expressed my intention of writing an investigatory book on the religions of India, he not only stated encouragingly that the project was most suitable but also advised me on matters relating to its planning and execution.

During the last few decades Chetana has been rendering a commendable service to readers in different countries by publishing various writings in the fields of religion and philosophy. Many publications of Chetana relating to J. Krishnamurti, the religious revolutionary teacher of our times, are especially noteworthy. Evaluative studies of Krishnamurti's teachings have been published in the *Krishnamurti Library* series. Furthermore, certain rare and out-of-print works by Krishnamurti have also been reprinted.

In the present book there are quite a few passing references to Krishnamurti, but for more detailed investigations into his teachings, readers are requested to peruse the following works of mine which were all published by Chetana: *Living and Dying from Moment to Moment* (1978), *Supplement to A Bibliography of the Life and Teachings of Jiddu Krishnamurti* (1982), *That Pathless Land* (1983) and *Bliss of Reality* (1984).

Professor E.F.C. Ludowyk very carefully revised my manuscript and I must record my deep appreciation of his invaluable assistance.

EDITOR'S NOTE

Numerous books have been written on the religions of India by various authors, but the present work is entirely different from them both in conception and presentation. We have read long and learned dissertations from erudite scholars discussing the dialectics and semantics of Indian religions as also their ontology and epistemology. We have also read comparative studies constructing and demolishing critical comments and arguments about these religions.

Susunaga Weeraperuma, the author of *Major Religions of India*, however, steers clear of all polemics. He does not assume the role of a critic nor that of a follower. His approach is totally neutral. He has no preconceived notions about the four major religions of India — Hinduism, Jainism, Buddhism and Sikhism — which he presents in this book without the least identification with the ideas and ideals propagated by them. With an alert and open mind he tries to understand what each of these religions stands for and summarizes in barest essentials what he has understood, thus making the book an epitome of brevity, simplicity and lucidity, an ideal introduction for the average modern reader who is eager to have a true understanding of the major Indian religions, without cluttering his mind with abstruse philosphical terminology.

This apart, what, in my view, will appeal most to the reader of this book is the strong streak of rationality in the author's presentation of his subject. While placing before the readers the crux and kernel of each religion with complete impartiality, he puts forward, in between, certain rational questions about a few of their beliefs and dogmas. These are the questions which any present-day intellectual would like to be answered satisfactorily. For example, while dealing with Hinduism, the most major of Indian religions, he finds himself unable to accept the theory that there are different paths to reach God.

The basic assumption is that God *is* and that he is somewhere where he could be reached. I may recall here the momentous words of W.T. Stace in his *Religion and Modern Man*. Referring to the unprovability of the existence of God he says: "If God does not lie at the end of a telescope, neither does he lie at the end of any syllogism". The general belief of most religions is that there prevails a 'divine order' as also a 'natural order'. While belief in the latter is a matter of proof, belief in the former is a product of faith. Logically also, when we see the phantasmagoria of the creation around us, we conclude that there must be a creator of this creation. Assuming that God *was* the creator of the world, can we not assume that after he created it, the laws of gravitation and motion took over the world's functioning, just as in the case of a watch which runs automatically by its own internal mechanism, after the watchmaker has made it. But then it may be asserted that God created the natural laws also. The question would then arise as to who created God.

The author is a modern intellectual and a free thinker. Vague and woolly assumptions are an anathema to him. In his chapter on Hinduism he challenges the theory that there are different ways of reaching God. This reminds me of the old philosophical conundrum: How many angels can dance on the head of a pin? This question is inherently unanswerable, for while the size of the pinhead is known, nobody knows how big or small the angels are, or whether they exist at all, for nobody is known to have seen them. Says the author:

> "The theory that there are different ways of reaching God presupposes that God is approachable. But can the limited, finite and conditioned mind of man ever approach that which is limitless, infinite and unconditioned?... Can the known find that which is totally unknown via the known?"

The conclusion that God *is* and that he is located somewhere where he can be reached by treading the right path, is similar to the dancing of angles on a pinhead!

Further, discussing the Bhakti-Marga (path of devotion) he is at a loss to understand as to how one can fall in love with someone who is an absolutely unknown and unseen entity — a mere abstraction, namely God. He feels that the devotees of God or gods are engaged in the dovotion of mere psychological images of their deities that they have formed in their minds either by themselves or under the influence of their teachers. "Is not the worship of an image that thrives in the mind a kind of self-worship?" he questions. He goes on to say:

> "The ingenious Hindu mind, alas, invented gods — gods who exist nowhere except in the private worlds of fantasy of their devotees."

Such snide remarks apart, we must admit that the author has drawn a faithful sketch of Hinduism and explained tersely its major doctrines with exemplary clarity and brevity.

The Godlessness of Jainism and Buddhism has saved them from the fanciful flights of imagination in which the Hindu Bhaktas indulge with unbounded zeal. These two religions do not have any transcendental doctrines or beliefs in a supernatural realm tenanted by deities.

However, in his chapter on Jainism the rationalist in the author cannot help pointing out the utter impracticability of some of the Jain practices, which they consider sacred. For example, the austerities imposed on the Jain Munis appear to him atrocious, almost suicidal. He also questions the Jain doctrine of Ahimsa, as he finds it beyond the bounds of reason and totally unperformable. The willful destruction of life could be and should be avoided, he says, but the fruits and vegetables that the Jains eat are also forms of life. In fact "every atom is pervaded by life . . . the Jain doctrine of Ahimsa cannot be fully and faithfully observed, unless one totally gives up not only eating and drinking, but breathing as well. It would seem that the only logical course open to the truly devout Jain is to opt to die", he concludes.

In his chapter on Buddhism the author seems to be comparatively more at ease. While presenting the essentials of Buddhism he admires in glowing terms the Buddha's dictum that man is his own saviour and there is no 'divine decree' that he has to follow. There is no God to be appeased and there is no divine being to listen to man's prayers. Truth is its own proof. As in the case of the other religions that the author deals with, he does not put forward any questions that the Buddhists may find embarrassing to answer.

In the chapter on Sikhism, however, the author is baffled by certain irrationalities. Sikhism, the youngest religion of India, started as an offshoot of the mediaeval Vaishnava mysticism of Bhakti Marga, but soon developed a theology of its own which is a sort of hybrid growth of Vaishnavism and Islam. It retained the Bhakti Marga, but eschewed the concept of gods and deities and totally rejected idol-worship. Its conception of God is predominantly Islamic, as the great provider and helper who knows the needs of all men and provides them accordingly. Elsewhere, however, God is also described as having "neither any form nor material sign." In the Adi Granth there is a hymn in which God is described almost in Vedantic terms as "pure and without beginning, changeless; the same from age to age."

These different definitions of God are rather confusing, but the confusion gets worse confounded when Guru Nanak, the founder of Sikhism, avers: "God Himself created Himself." The author pounces down on the pronouncement and questions: How come this happened? Did God exist prior to His birth?

The cardinal principle of Sikhism is complete surrender to God. Nanak says:

> "He who submits to God's will is accepted and treasured by him... Whatever God wills, that occurs, for nothing is in the hands of man. All are yoked to God's will, and will be judged according to their deeds."

The author is skeptical about these dictates. He questions:

> "If my will were always overpowered by that of God... then why should I be held responsible for my deeds? ... If God were in total control over man, then should we be blamed for anything 'sinful' that we do? ... What is the point of exhorting man to *submit* himself to the will of God, unless he were capable of volition himself?"

Nanak further asserts: "He alone is dear to God who

utters his name . . . Dwell only on God's name, all other deeds are fruitless."

Nanak's one-pointed sole emphasis on *nam japa*, the constant repetition of God's name, provokes the author into debunking the so-called mystical experiences of the God-intoxicated devotees as mere self-hypnosis. He argues:

> "Through the constant repetition of any word, regardless of whether that word is 'sacred', 'profane', 'obscene' or even meaningless, an artificial state of stillness can certainly be induced . . . the stream of consciousness . . . gets temporarily halted because of this kind of self-hypnosis and the resultant short-lived quietness is mistakenly called 'bliss' . . . In this state one experiences 'visions' of God . . . The 'God' one sees is nothing more than the mind's own creations . . . The mind can only see what has already been lurking within it . . . We see in 'visions' what we have been unconsciously longing to see. Thus the Catholic experiences a 'vision' of the Virgin . . . Similarly, the Shaivite saints had 'visions' of Lord Shiva . . ."

Further, the author asks, rather innocently: "If the repetition of God's name is the condition to be fulfilled whereby man endears himself to God, then must not God be rather vain?"

The author's chapter on Sikhism is indeed a battle of wits in which a modern intellectual seems to be combating with a mediaeval saint. But as a piece of writing the chapter is as serious as it is entertaining.

When Weeraperuma's manuscript came to me for editing I greatly enjoyed reading it, without, of course, agreeing with him in all that he says. At times I felt that the author was perhaps too logical-minded to be able to appreciate or apprehend the mystic experiences of Bhaktas. These experiences are of the nature of in-seeing or intuitive seeing, in contradistinction to analytical understanding. The words and expressions used by a Bhakta are not denotative but evocative. The author is perhaps incapable of realizing that intuition is something beyond intellection and that apart from the senses and the mind there could also be some other instrument of cognition.

Weeraperuma, I know for certain, is steeped deeply in the philosophy of J. Krishnamurti, the arch questioner and doubter of the present century. And, like his mentor, he questions and doubts. There is no wonder that rituals appear to him as meaningless fuss, prayers as mere exercises in auto-suggestion and the 'visions' of God as mere projections of one's own unconscious imaginings. And all these, he believes, lead to an irremediable conditioning of the mind.

Personally I think that to absorb on a subliminal level the thoughts of others is conditioning of the mind and to see through the patterns of conditioning is true learning.

Does Weeraperuma in this work see through the doctrines and dogmas of the religions he has dealt with? Let the readers decide on this point.

The wise old Bacon observed: "He that questioneth much, shall learn much." And Weeraperuma does question much, no doubt.

Sudhakar S. Dikshit
Editor

CONTENTS

I
HINDUISM

Hinduism is not a static body of doctrine: it is rather a living, dynamic and ever-growing religion, its adherents forming the largest number of India's population. It eludes definition because its literature is so wide in range that it includes many diverse points of view, beliefs and dogmas. Within its fold are persons who subscribe to teachings that are diametrically opposed: theism and polytheism on the one hand; and atheism on the other. The grossest superstitions and the profoundest philosophical insights exist cheek by jowl in the complex and commodious house of Hinduism. When a religion consists, among other things, of the mystical outpourings of multitudinous sages over several millennia, and the mythical and legendary tales of a people with a fertile imagination, it becomes risky for any writer to define it precisely. It borders on the indefinable. The best he can safely do is to examine objectively just some of its salient features so that the reader is helped to draw his own conclusions.

All the various ideas and beliefs that constitute Hinduism are not contained in any single sacred book, as in the case of the Koran, the foundational scripture of Islam, nor were they pronounced by a single prophet. Apart from the Vedas and the Upanishads, there is an immense ocean of Hindu religious literature in which one can easily founder. One wonders whether any scholar would find even an entire lifetime sufficient for studying all the written texts of Hinduism, let alone the various esoteric instructions and traditions that have been orally transmitted.

Freedom from thought

Hinduism maintains that the Self, which is the source of all creativity, is within oneself. Many make the mistake of regarding the Self as some kind of external object that has to be laboriously sought and found. But when one looks within and realizes the Self, it will be seen that one is not different from the universe but is oneself the universe. All sense of illusory separation between oneself and the universe totally disappears.

According to the Mandukyopanishad, what is commonly called the waking state of consciousness comes into being when perception is turned outwards. In this state the Self enjoys the experience of contact with coarse matter. But what is known as the dream state arises when perception is focussed inwards, when the Self enjoys contact with thought, which is nothing but a kind of subtle matter.

The person who is awake should be differentiated from the person who is dreaming on the basis of the direction in which his perception has been channelled. In other words, when our sense organs have been stimulated, such as by the sight of something that is beautiful, the attention of the Self flows away from itself in an outward direction. But during the dream state, in contrast, the Self is not reacting to external stimuli but only to the contents of the unconscious. Here again the Self is running away from itself in the sense that it has become entangled in the thoughts that lurk in the hidden layers of the mind. In both the waking and the dream states, the Self is not aware of itself because it has been distracted by predominantly external and internal stimuli respectively.

There is, however, the state of dreamless sleep when the Self is undisturbed by stimuli, internal or external. This is a state without thought and hence an intensely restful, peaceful and joyous one. In this exalted state there is total absorption in the Self, for the Self is, as it were, enjoying its own bliss. By its very nature this state must always remain indescribable: it is unthinkable because the moment thought comes in, its inherent purity is vitiated. Its purity consists in its essential freedom from all thought.

Through the instrumentality of thought the Self can never be realized. The Self and thought are mutually exclusive. When the intelligence of the Self is shining in all its splendour, thought finds itself totally immobilised; but when thought is active, the Self is temporarily eclipsed, although it is always there, eternal and indestructible. It will be seen that between thought and the Self there can be no relationship whatsoever.

This point is so well conveyed in the immortal words of the Kenopanishad:

> "Mind reaches not there, nor does sight,
> And speech knows not its silent bliss;
> That which is beyond all knowing
> What words can describe its glory?"

In our so-called modern civilization an inordinate importance has unfortunately been given to thought. Undoubtedly, thought has its many uses, and deserves its rightful place in human affairs. Organized thought, in the form of language, is necessary because it is our principal means of communication; thought enables us to record and recall whatever is worth remembering. It is the thought process that has made possible all our literature and culture as well as the tremendous advances in science and technology. Despite all such benefits, we must also realize that thought is at best only an useful tool. So long as thought remains our servant, and not our master, we can live intelligently. For all the psychological problems of man are traceable to his thought process. It is only in the fertile soil of thought that the poisonous weeds of hatred, malice, jealousy, fear and suspicion thrive. The evil of racism, which is one of the most disruptive forces in the modern world, not only originates in thought but is also nurtured and propagated by thought. Nevertheless, when using thought, as we unavoidably must do in our daily lives, we should never lose touch with what the Upanishads call the Self, that realm of non-intellectual perception, which is the source of all clarity, creativity and spiritual felicity.

Roads to Realization

The belief that there are many roads to spiritual salvation is a source of great psychological solace and happiness for Hindus. A modern exponent of this belief was Sri Ramakrishna Paramhamsa, who maintained that all religions are just diverse paths leading to God, in the same way that all the rivers coming from different directions ultimately merge and become one in the vast ocean. For him the names of God are many, and infinite are the forms through which God could be approached. Sri Ramakrishna declared:

> "In whatever name and form you worship Him, through that He will be realized by you."

Hinduism as a religion is extraordinarily tolerant of every point of view, because of the commonly shared intuitive feeling of its followers that all paths lead finally to the same goal of spiritual salvation. Hinduism may be likened to a sponge with an inexhaustible capacity to absorb many different creeds. Consequently, religious fanaticism, the practice of persecution for heresy or engagement in *jehads* or holy wars, are all contrary to its basic character. The person who meditates in solitude is extended the same tolerance that is accorded to the Sadhu who may perform any strange eccentricities, such as standing on one leg for an indefinite period in the hope that he might thereby somehow find the release of *mukti* (liberation).

The Hindu theory that there are different paths for reaching the Truth or God presupposes that God is approachable. But can the limited, finite and conditioned mind of man ever approach that which is limitless, infinite and unconditioned? Can the mind, with the assis
tioning or karma. Therefore, when he follows the path
sphere of the unknown? Can the known find that which is totally unknown via the known? The mind can admittedly recognize what is already known to it, but is it capable of cognizing that which is outside the field of knowledge and therefore unimaginable? It would seem that the Absolute is not cognizable by the severely restricted instrument of the intellect. It would appear that Truth is a "pathless land", as J. Krishnamurti says and you cannot approach it by any path whatsoever.

When a person finds himself drawn to a particular spiritual path and then decides to follow it through and through, his decision would have been determined solely by his temperament and psychological background. But one's temperament and psychological background; or, in other words, the way the mind has been conditioned, constitutes one's Karma. So when a person having been attracted to, say, Bhakti Marga (the path of devotion), wishes to pursue it, he is not acting freely by any means, but is merely reacting to the particular inclination of his own mind. In the name of spirituality, alas, he is only reacting mechanically in full accordance with the dictates of his own psychological conditioning or Karma. Therefor, when he follows the path of his own choosing, is he not just reinforcing his

Karma, instead of extricating himself from it? Is he not, in other words, strengthening the particular psychological groove within which he is already operating by getting himself caught up in its threads? Nevertheless, despite the aforementioned objections, let us *assume* that spiritual paths are necessary, and proceed to discuss some of the well-known paths that have been prescribed in Hinduism.

Several means have been recommended for attaining union with the Divine so that the sense of separate individuality ceases to exist altogether. One of the meanings of the word *yoga* is the joining of the particular principle with the general principle, the individual soul with the Oversoul, the Divine, or, the merging of the spark with the flame from which the spark originated, so that ultimately there is only oneness or completeness. The different paths leading to the realization of God have been traditionally known as:

Bhakti-Yoga (the path of devotion)
Karma-Yoga (the path of action)
Jnāna-Yoga (the path of knowledge)
Rāja-Yoga (the path of insight)

The Path of Devotion (*Bhakti-Yoga*)

Bhakti is the effulgent state when the heart and mind are full of intense devotion to Vishnu, Shiva or any of the numerous gods of the Hindu pantheon. Bhakti is composed of several elements, such as deep love for the god in question as well as undeviating faith in him; the willingness to surrender oneself entirely to the deity, and the unswerving belief in the ability of that god to provide protection and salvation for all his devotees fully committed to serving him. Perhaps the best example of such devotion was that of Rādhā to her beloved Krishna.

Hindu literature is replete with expressions of absolute love of the devotees for various deities. The spirit of Bhakti is epitomized in the following words of Nammālvār, a Bhakta poet:

> "My Lord, though ceaseless pains trouble me, I will never stop looking for your mercy."

A profound description of the nature of Bhakti is given in the *Aphorisms of Sāndilya*, a classic of Bhakti-Marga. Some of these aphorisms paraphrased by me, given below, have been intermixed with my own comments. Bhakti is not knowledge although it may be the consequence of knowledge. Even the atheists who hate the god that is adored, are, in fact, themselves devotees, because their hatred really springs from their hidden, and perhaps unconscious, recognition of the power of the deity. A similar sentiment was expressed by Rabindranath Tagore:

> "I am able to love my God because He gives me freedom to deny Him."

A worshipper is not necessarily a devotee because worship can also originate in fear, as it so often does. Worshipping is an outward act that may be devoid of that element of tenderness, unqualified and undiluted affection, which constitutes Bhakti. Bhakti is pure and selfless love for the deity. It is not to be found in someone whose deeds depend on the exercise of will. For the presence of will indicates that the ego or the self is still active, whereas the deeds of a pure devotee are utterly selfless. Works become pure only if the doer truly surrenders them to the deity. No action is pure unless it is god-orientated and is performed as a sacrifice. Respecting, honouring and praising the deity, who is the object of one's adorations, are manifestations of Bhakti.

A psychological trait noticeable in the many Bhaktas

whom I have met is their lack of interest in meditation as a means of actually having firsthand, direct and personal contact with the gods whom they adore. They are not keen on knowing whether their favourite gods belong to the realms of fact or fiction. They seem strangely satisfied with the mere *belief* that their gods somehow exist somewhere. That belief psychologically sustains them; it helps them through the various vicissitudes of life. The associated belief that their gods have their welfare at heart assists them to overcome feelings of depression and hopelessness. It fills their hearts and minds with optimism, although they are living in a world full of sorrows and sufferings and is threatened by the disaster of nuclear war!

One of the easiest ways of disturbing the smug security and self-satisfaction of Bhaktas is by showing disrespect for their deities. They strongly resent the people who make fun of their gods. Sometimes Bhaktas avoid associating with non-believers, also they never entertain thoughts that are unrelated to their gods lest their faith is threatened. Bhakti Marga mainly appeals to those persons who are temperamentally very emotional. Bhaktas are often moved to tears during the course of chanting hymns in honour of their gods. Such is the intensity of feeling they have for their beloved gods. But Bhaktas are usually unaware that by thus discharging their pent-up emotions, they are only helping themselves to restore their psychological equilibrium and composure.

One of the best expositions of Bhakti-Marga is contained in the *Bhagavadgita*, popularly regarded as the most sacred book in the Hindu world. Certain passages in this work give the impression that it has a definite bias towards the path of devotion. Lord Krishna, the spokesman of the Divine, who is also regarded as the Divine itself, makes these revelations:

> "Four kinds of virtuous men render devotional service unto Me — the distressed, the desirer of knowledge, the man seeking wealth and he who is imbued with wisdom.
>
> "Of these persons, the best is the wise one who is in full union with Me through pure devotional service. For I am very dear to him, and he is dear to Me.
>
> "He who adheres to this imperishable path of devotional service and who totally engages himself with faith, making Me the supreme goal, is very, very dear to Me."

It is reasonable to suppose that Bhakti naturally flowers in the hearts of those seers who were fortunate enough to have experienced a beatific vision of the Absolute. They are capable of loving God and being devoted to him because they have already known God. It is certainly possible to love something about which you already have knowledge. But is it really possible to love something about which you are entirely ignorant? I can love a person whom I may have met only once, but is it possible to fall in love with one totally unknown, a mere abstraction, namely God? This is the principal difficulty with Bhakti Marga.

The other criticism is that those who commit their lives to the path of devotion, whose adoration is directed to a deity or to God, usually end up by being worshippers of mere psychological images. For example, every time a Saivite offers *puja* to Lord Shiva, is he in actual communion with that deity in person; or, is he merely making obeisance to the mental picture of Shiva as it exists in his imagination? That psychological image may or may not have all the reported trappings of Shiva, such as his trident or skull-garland, but it still remains a figment of the imagination of a person who never saw Shiva face-to-face. And is not the worship of an image that thrives in the mind a kind of self-worship? This criticism can also be levelled against the practice of adoring the other hundreds of deities who constitute the Hindu pantheon. The ingenious Hindu mind, alas, invented gods who exist nowhere except in the private worlds of fantasy of their devotees. These inventions have enslaved the minds of millions throughout the ages and even now continue to enslave the minds of those naive enough to believe in them.

The Path of Action (*Karma-Yoga*)

When all his actions are performed for the greater glory of the Lord, a spiritual aspirant is said to tread the path of Karma-Yoga. Nothing is done by him which is not a sacrificial act either directly or indirectly. Every act has a dedicatory purpose. In a sense, the paths of Bhakti-Yoga and Karma-Yoga are inextricably linked, because unless a person is ardently in love with the Lord, how can he ensure that all his actions spring from that devotional source? All the deeds of a pure Bhakta will be God-orientated anyway, and it can be argued that such a person need not bother with Karma-Yoga at all.

The *Bhagavadgita* explains very clearly the essence of Karma Yoga:

> "He who without attachment, resigning his actions to God, is untainted by sin, as the lotus leaf is untouched by water.
>
> "Abandoning the fruit of action he attains peace born of steadfastness, the non-Yogi is bound as he is attached to the fruit of action.

> "He who discharges his duty without seeking its fruit, he is the Sanyasi, he is the Yogi, not he who is without the sacred fire and without the rites."

The Karma-Yogi is emphatically enjoined to renounce what is called 'the fruits of action'. This simply means that a man should do his duty with a sense of total indifference to the rewards that might accrue from his actions. All he is concerned with is working to the best of his ability. The sheer excellence of his work might result in his rising high in the estimation of society. But he remains indifferent to praise and fame. The compliments of his admirers do not inflate his ego. On the other hand, if he becomes the target of criticism and ridicule because he has bungled his work, even in such circumstances he remains indifferent to the insults and opprobrium of the world. However, the chances of blundering by someone, who is so pure in heart and so untarnished in mind, would probably be remote.

The anonymous painters and sculptors, who helped to adorn some of the ancient temples of India, including places such as Ajanta and Ellora, with works of art of such exquisite beauty, were probably Karma-Yogis at heart, insofar as they were inspired solely by their love of the Supreme.

Do the selfless deeds of those social welfare workers of our time, who tirelessly try to uplift the living conditions of the poor and destitute in the slums of big cities, fall into the category of Karma-Yoga? These persons sacrifice their precious time and energy and expose themselves to numerous hardships, but they receive no earthly reward for all their efforts. Although many of them are undoubtedly inspired by compassion, still they are not recognized as Karma-Yogis only because their activities do not apparently take the form of a sacred offering to God. A true Karma-Yogi is utterly selfless and wholly dedicated to his work. He is not a slave to any desires. And slavery is of different kinds. There is the slavery of a subject people who have to bear the crushing burden of a tyrannical form of government; there is the humiliating slavery of a helpless employee who is at the mercy of a ruthless employer. But the worst form of slavery is being the lifelong prisoner of one's own psychological compulsions. Our psychological traits make us what we are. Without these traits there would be no ego for the self is constituted of one's unresolved conflicts, hopes, fears, sorrows and the like. All the work that a person does becomes the expression of that self, his ego with its incessant demands for power, recognition and so forth. So long as this self is in existence, the quality of the work that is performed must surely get marred. But during those rare moments, when the self is temporarily inactive, one gets directed by some inexplicable power, which may be called God for the want of a better word. And one becomes an instrument in the hands of that indescribable power which operates only when the self is not operating.

In the light of what has been said, it is clear that only the person who has discarded his self is truly qualified to become a Karma-Yogi. For the selfless acts of a Karma-Yogi are pure and *karmaless*. In a sense, therefore, the state of Karma-Yoga should not be regarded as a means to an end but rather as the end itself. The Karma-Yogi loses the self and finds the Self.

The Path of Knowledge (*Jnāna-Yoga*)

A profound truth of Hinduism is enshrined in a great and pithy saying from the Upanishads, which conveys the essence of Jnāna-Yoga. This *mahāvākya* is no other than *tat-tvam-asi*, which means 'That thou art'. The full realization of what is termed 'That' is the be-all and end-all of Jnāna-Yoga.

One of our greatest difficulties is that we have become attached to our thought processes which, by their very nature, are unstable and changeable. The stream of consciousness is ever in a state of perpetual flux because thoughts keep on cropping up and disappearing all the time. Except during the state of dreamless sleep, this river of consciousness is always flowing, slowly or rapidly, never knowing a moment of stillness. So when we identify ourselves with our thoughts, we not only tend to get carried away by them, but we become oblivious to the fact that this changeable thought process is only a mere superimposition upon that substratum of pure consciousness, which alone is changeless and deathless. This impermanent and fluctuating mind may be likened to a dark shadow which has been cast upon an everlasting and indestructible substratum — the state of pure consciousness, or the Self. And if we fail to become aware of the existence of that substratum, which is always there, is it not because of our preoccupation with the things of the mind? If it were possible to cast aside the entire machinery of the intellect, even for a few fleeting seconds, would we not get a glimpse of that which lies beyond the reach of the mind? Then one would realize the great truth that one's essential state of being is neither the ephemeral mind nor the perishable body, but 'That', which is variously named as the 'Self', 'pure consciousness' or '*Brahman*'.The Jnāni is the enlightened person who has shed the illusory world of thought and has thereby discovered that cosmic consciousness, the realization of which is epitomized by the saying 'That thou art'.

Let us consider a person engrossed in the enjoyment of a film picturising a graceful dancer. His attention gets concentrated upon the rhythmic movements of the dancer that appear on the screen in the form of very rapidly moving photographic images. When he gets enraptured by what he sees, he becomes forgetful of the existence of the screen. Now, but for the prior presence of the white blank screen, could those images have been seen at all? Yet his engrossment with the images is such that he overlooks the prime importance and indispensability of the screen without which he could not have seen the film.

Similarly, our psychological images are focussed onto the screen of pure consciousness, or the Self. The activities of the mind may be likened to an endless dance on the screen of the Self. The mind is the illusory and variable factor whereas the Self remains constant

It is not that a Jñani is disinclined to employ thought for the reason that thought is transitory and deceptive. In his mundane everyday activities he may make use of thought, but he never gets attached to it; and immediately after using it as an instrument, his awareness reverts to the Self, the Real, the Actual, which is the abode within which he always dwells. Once a Jñani becomes aware of the Self and realizes that the Self alone is deathless, the eternal noumenon behind all phenomenality, that extraordinary discovery is never lost. Thenceforth his entire life starts radiating from that eternal source.

The Path of Insight (*Rāja-Yoga*)

Rāja-Yoga, 'the King of Yogas', is mainly concerned with self-inquiry and meditation and self-discipline as the royal road to spiritual illumination. Naturally, the embarkation on such an inner voyage of investigation appeals only to a few. It is widely regarded as the hardest of the paths.

The view that the mind is a spiritual substance is fallacious because it is entirely composed of matter howsoever rarefied. The mind is only a subtle form of matter, though it may seem otherwise to the superficial observer. When we immerse ourselves in thought we remain in the realm of matter only, for all thought is manifestation of mind which is a manifestation of matter, therefore we have to ask ourselves this vital question: Is it possible to tanscend this materialistic thought process and enter into a dimension that is purely spiritual or totally non-materialistic? There are various recommended practices that have as their sole objective the transition from the sphere of matter to that of the spirit.

One of these is the Āstānga-Yoga (eightfold path of discipline) expounded by. Patanjali: The eight steps recommended by Patanjali are:

(1) Yama
(2) Niyama
(3) Āsana
(4) Prānāyāma
(5) Pratyāhāra
(6) Dhāranā
(7) Dhyāna
(8) Samādhi

Now let us critically examine these eight rungs of the ladder of spiritual progress:

Yama

Yamas are five in number: *Ahimsa* (non-violence), *Satya* (truthfulness), *Asteya* (honesty), *Brahmacharya* (sensual abstinence), and *Aparigraha* (non-acquisitiveness).

The novice assiduously practises *ahimsa* by not injuring any living creature. He ensures that all his thoughts, words and deeds are non-injurious.

He does not utter any falsehood. By abstaining from

lying, *satya*, one is of course preventing oneself from deceiving others. Yet such a restraint is no safeguard against self-deception. The ego likes to cherish delusions of its own grandeur and feel that it is somehow spiritually evolving so that it eventually merges into the Absolute.

He refrains from dishonesty (*asteya*). Whereas it is comparatively easy to be honest in relation to transactions involving money or material goods, it is far more difficult to be true to oneself. The mind has a great capacity for deception which is often overlooked. We fail to see the unconscious motives that govern our behaviour. A statesman, for instance, who talks endlessly about the need for social justice and world peace, may lack the honesty to admit that he is not really interested in any of these things but is merely seeking his own personal profit and glory.

A man tries to subdue his passions and lust (*brahmacharya*). But it may be questioned that he who tries to repress a 'troublesome' or 'objectionable' emotion or thought will find that it will emerge again, sooner or later, and often with greater force. The harder one strikes a rubber ball the more it bounces. The mind cannot be quietened by fighting unruly feelings and thoughts. On the other hand, if the stream of thoughts and feelings is passively watched, without any sense of censorship or approval, the state of tranquillity comes about unexpectedly.

Non-acquisitiveness is more than overcoming avarice. It is not only non-possessiveness, but losing the sense of possession even of what you happen to possess. Even a yearning for liberation is a desire to acquire and possess. There is no fundamental difference between the greed for wealth and the passionate thirst for God. The ideal of *aparigraha* as laid out by Patanjali is indeed very difficult to attain.

Niyama

Niyamas also are five in number: cleanliness (*shaucha*), contentment (*santosh*), austerity (*tapas*), self-study (*svādhyāya*) and resignation to God (*Iswara-pranidhana*).

The devotee is expected to take steps towards his self-improvement by being pure, contented and austere as well as by self-study. When a person who is devoid of purity, contentment, austerity or indeed any virtue for that matter, tries to acquire them, what happens? Does not the mind immediately get enslaved by the snare of duality? Does not the becoming process come into operation when the state of *what is* tries vainly to become the state of what *should be*? When an impure mind speculates about 'purity', that so-called ideal of purity which it invents and then tries to emulate, is essentially a product and a projection of its own latent impurity. That ideal is the pathological and artificial creation of a mind which is already disturbed by impure thoughts. With the coin of impurity we want to buy purity! The quality of impurity can never alter itself into purity any more than hate can ever undergo a sea change and suddenly become love. Hate will always remain hate and the same thing can also be said of impurity. However, if the existence of impurity were faced fully, honestly acknowledged and all its deleterious implications and consequences completely understood, then it will surely disappear of its own accord. When the autumnal leaves of impurity fall down effortlessly, purity blooms automatically.

In addition to these the devotee is also required to be devoted to the Supreme (*Ishwara-pranidhana*). The question is not whether he should be devoted, but whether, given his conditioned and unrealized state, can he ever be so devoted? A devotee is someone who is still in the process of finding the truth. Is he therefore capable of being devoted to something that is obviously outside his field of experience? How can a person possibly venerate that which is unknown?

Asana

There are an estimated eighty-four *āsanas* or bodily postures but only some of them are chosen for meditation. A person is free to select those postures in which he can remain comfortably for the greatest length of time. Patanjali thought that an *āsana* should be *sthira-sukhaṁ* (firm and comfortable).

It is believed that certain thoughts are best developed by certain *āsanas* which should be performed while facing a given direction.

Some Hatha-Yogis regard the practising of *āsanas* as an end in itself. There is a great joy in having a perfect body and in vigilantly maintaining that perfection. Yet there are others for whom these practices are only a means to keeping the organism reasonably healthy, supple, sensitive and energetic. Through the regular performance of these exercises the ageing process can be slowed. But the orthodox view is that the practice of *āsanas* is only a preparatory step in the journey towards spiritual emancipation. Consequently there is a tendency to frown upon those who practise Hatha-Yoga with the intention of acquiring supernatural powers or *siddhis*, such as the ability to levitate. *Siddhis* become a distraction for a person who is seriously trying to understand the ways of the self, and thereby leave no room for any of its subtle manifestations. For a person who has laboriously acquired supernatural powers will probably be so proud of his accomplishments that he might be tempted to parade them in public, in the same way that some like to show off their material wealth.

If we agree that true meditation consists in the constant awareness of one's psychological reactions to persons, ideas, inanimate objects, situations and so forth, then we have to question the claim that *āsanas* are an indispensable aid to meditation. One can surely watch the mind in operation at any given moment of the day and not merely when practising *padmāsana* or *siddhāsana*. The hidden contents of the unconscious may unexpectedly surface when one is travelling in a taxi or having a bath. However, I have found that the body becomes so relaxed while engaged in *āsanas*, as well as afterwards, that the movements of the mind can be watched with a certain undivided attention, especially because one is no longer distracted by muscular tensions. *Āsanas* are thus an indirect physical aid to self-observation.

Prāṇāyāma

Ordinarily the word *prāna* refers to the breath or the life-force. It is the continuous action of breathing in and out that enables the body to be constantly supplied with oxygen without which we cannot survive. But the Yogis attach to that word a certain esoteric meaning, besides the simple involuntary process of inhalation and exhalation. According to them *prāna* is the mysterious primordial energy that animates the entire universe. Therefore the longer one is able to retain air in the lungs after inhaling it, the more one partakes of that vital power. Untrained persons breathe haphazardly but the Yogis practise various techniques which enables them not only to breathe deeply but also to regulate the duration of the three elements of *prānāyāma* — the inhalation, retention and exhalation of the breath.

As one who regularly practises *prānāyāma* every morning, I know from personal experience how right breathing invigorates the body. One feels tremendously energetic after every session of breathing exercises.

Certain very old Yogis whom I encountered in my travels attributed their longevity purely to the practice of *prāṇāyāma*. One Yogi remarked that it was the vitality of *prāṇa* that supported his life and not the meagre food he ate.

Some Hindu savants identify *prāṇa* with Brahman and carefully cultivate certain thoughts when practising deep breathing exercises. As the air fills their lungs they imagine that God is mysteriously entering into their bodies, and then leaving it afterwards as they slowly exhale. Since retaining the breath can become arduous, they console themselves by thinking that they are, at least for a short time, seizing the divine power. Totally oblivious of the understanding that the Infinite is beyond the comprehension of the finite mind, they visualize God as though he were some kind of temporary visitor who can be forcibly held.

Pratyāhāra

When the mind gets fascinated by what is experienced via the sense organs, it tends to move in an outward direction instead of inwards, towards the Self. In the same way as when a child finds a toy of such absorbing interest that it becomes unaware of the existence of everything else, ordinary persons, too, get distracted by various sensory stimuli, whereas a Yogi tries to be completely indifferent to such stimuli so that his attention could be engrossed in his inner spiritual world at all times.

In this connection an interesting incident in the early life of Ramana Maharshi is worth mentioning here because it illustrates the rare state of consciousness that *pratyāhāra* generates. The young Swami was once doing penance is a dark pit of Mount Arunachala. He was in a state of deep meditation, wholly absorbed in the Infinite. It is reported that his body was attacked by scorpions, ants, mosquitoes and other vermin that bit him and sucked his blood. Consequently there were sores all over his body. But he remained completely unaware of his physical condition. He was then in the state of *pratyāhāra*, when the mind was totally withdrawn from all sense-experience.

Dhāranā

Inspired by the belief that it is necessary to have a mind capable of intense concentration, various techniques have been advocated. All these have the single aim of achieving what is called 'one-pointedness of mind'.

There are two practices that are common to all the systems of concentration: first, one selects the object of concentration, such as the tip of one's nose, the space between the eyebrows, a mark or a symbol on a wall or the statue or picture of a deity; second, one endeavours to focus the mind solely on the chosen object of concentration and exclude all intruding thoughts.

What generally happens when the mind attempts to concentrate on any particular thing? No sooner does one manage to concentrate for a few seconds than there suddenly arises a flood of extraneous thoughts. The thought process is very intricate, obstinate and insubordinate; it cannot be tamed by any exercise of will. Then begins the battle for supremacy between the 'desired thought' and the 'undesired thoughts'. The mind is reduced to a sort of boxing ring of conflicting forces where there is neither clarity nor peace.

A matter often overlooked is that the 'I', the agency that tries to regulate thought, is itself a thought. The 'I'-thought says "I will have only this particular thought and no other in the mind". When the 'I' tries to eliminate all undesirable thoughts', and if temporarily succeeds in doing so, it naturally acquires a sense of its own importance and power. One of the unfortunate psychological side-effects of this practice is the emergence of an enormously strengthened ego.

Why brush aside any thought? If a thought keeps on recurring, one might as well welcome it as one would a long-lost friend, and then allow that thought to express itself to the full. When all the hidden aspects of a thought have been unreservedly exposed to the searching light of awareness, can it be a disturbing factor any more? It is not by chasing away 'undesirable thoughts' but by being aware of their presence, without any sense of hostility, that the state of tranquillity is realized. It is the peaceful mind alone that can focus its undivided attention on anything, without any struggle whatsoever. Great is the beauty of such a mind because of its natural ability to concentrate effortlessly.

Dhyāna

Meditation (*dhyāna*) is generally looked upon as the ability to concentrate uninterruptedly on whatever has been selected as the object of such concentration. There is much more to meditation than simply affixing the mind to whatever is fancied. Meditation includes a host of other abilities such as those concerned with seeing the ramifications of an issue, reading between the lines, and most importantly, getting into the heart of a question intuitively. Meditation is the process of emptying the mind of its psychological imagery. It is not suggested in the least that the mind should be cleansed of its accumulated knowledge because knowledge is indispensably necessary. But can we not throw away all the psychological imagery of a lifetime relating to our fears, hates, frustrations, aversions, likes, dislikes, ambitions, anxieties and so forth? When the mind is cluttered with such imagery, does it not lose the capacity to respond intelligently and quickly? When the mind is distracted because of its preoccupation with psychological problems, does it not become rather unobservant and insensitive? As a mountaineer must travel lightly, casting aside those things that are weighty and unnecessary for his ardous journey to the summit, so also must the mind be unburdened of its garbage of imagery, thus permitting it to soar to the heights of meditation.

Samādhi

According to H.P. Blavatsky, etymologically, the word *samādhi* means 'self-possession'. It is seen as the highest state of Yoga for in it one's whole consciousness is merged in the Self. Another meaning of this word is 'together (*sam*) with the Lord (*adhi*)'. It implies that one is in a state of perfect union with the vast and mysterious Unknown.

Samādhi is often described as an ecstatic trance. Such a statement, however, can neither be confirmed nor denied by the writer who has never experienced it. There is always the danger of indulging in speculation and then forming concepts about spiritual states that have not been personally known. It cannot be stated with certainty whether *samādhi*, once attained, is thenceforth continuous or intermittent. Probably it never leaves the person who has found spiritual freedom.

Elsewhere in this chapter we referred to the thought-free dimension of dreamless sleep, wherein there is complete absorption in the Self. The pure state of *samādhi*, too, is not only not contaminated by thought but there is in it also the experience of complete identification with the Self by whoever is enraptured by it. There is apparently no qualitative difference between the states of dreamless sleep and *samādhi*, except that the latter is experienced only when one is awake.

Perception gets distorted in both the dream state and the waking state of consciousness, because they are characterized invariably by a sense of division, duality or separateness. This division is caused by the 'I' or the 'observer', on the one hand; and the thing observed, on the other.

What is observed gets distorted according to the particular way in which the mind has been conditioned. We interpret every new experience in terms of our psychological backgrounds with the result that we never see or experience anything as it *actually is*. Our so-called seeing is necessarily biased because our minds have been moulded by countless influences, ideas, experiences and so forth. The 'observer' is the product of these conditioning factors. The 'observer' is the obstructive screen that stands in the way of direct contact with Reality. When the mischievous 'observer' is no more, then what happens? No longer the limitless ocean of Liberation is seen as being different from oneself, because one is already part and parcel of it. All sense of individuality disappears and one is conscious of being an integral and inseparable part of the Absolute.

Some writers have erroneously maintained that *samādhi* ensues when the 'I' is merged in the Divine, or, the subject unites with the object, as if the conditioned 'observer' were capable of combining with that which is Unconditioned! They have failed to realize that the self and the Unconditioned are utterly incompatible. It is only when the self dies that *samādhi* is born. *Samādhi*, it should be reiterated, is totally devoid of dualistic perception. When, for instance, the sky is gazed at during *samādhi*, there is never an 'I' that is looking at the sky: there is only the sky and nothing else in the field of perception. The immense sky is observed exactly as it *is*, without the intervention of the 'observer'. Hence *samādhi* is an extraordinary dimension of clarity, sanity and serenity.

However the four Yogas discussed above are not four separate paths leading to God, but four different attitudes towards Him. Love of God is Bhakti-Yoga; to serve God is Karma-Yoga; to see God everywhere, in all beings is Jnāna-Yoga and to realize God's complete identity with all that exists is Raja-Yoga. Actually all the different Hindu philosophies and apparently irreconcilable schools of thought have arisen out of one basic concept, namely the entire universe is a manifestation of God, who is immanent in all existence, but also transcends it. God is the impersonal or the supra-personal Absolute aspect of Truth. In himself he is Brahman or Satchidānanda. In relation to the universe, projected out of Himself, He is called Paramātma. When transcendent He is known as Isvara. In the masculine aspect He is Bhagavān. In the feminine form He is Bhagavati, variously called Devi, Durgā etc. Viewed in the different roles of the creator, protector and destroyer, He is named Brahmā, Vishnu and Shiva respectively. From these aspects and many more others emerged the baffling diversities of cults, creeds and sub-creeds which I have avoided discussing in this brief description of Hinduism.

The quintessence of Hinduism however is contained in the Upanishads which are the end parts of the Vedas. Of the six schools of Hindu philosophy, Vedānta and Yoga are supreme and the *Bhagavadgita* is the complete synthesis of all that forms the crux of Hinduism.

The supreme affirmation of the Upanishads is that of the total identity between the Atman and Brahman. When man comes to understand that he and the Infinite Spirit are one and the same, his *viveka* (spiritual consciousness) is awakened and *Vairāgya* (detachment from sense-pleasures) grows. He gets totally transformed from within and becomes a realized person, who has attained the summation and consummation of what is the highest teaching of Hinduism. Then there is nothing else to be attained. Having gained this state, says the *Bhagavadgita*, there is nothing greater to be gained, for this is the state in which even the heaviest affliction cannot shake anyone.

SELECT BIBLIOGRAPHY

ANDREWS, C.F. *The Renaissance in India: its Missionary Aspect.* London: Church Missionary Society, 1912

BANCROFT, Anne. *Religions of the East.* London: Heinemann, 1974

Bhagavad-Gita as it is, by A.C. Bhaktivedanta Swami Prabhupada New York: Macmillan, 1972

Encyclopaedia of Religion and Ethics; edited by James Hastings Edinburgh: T. & T. Clark, 1959

NARASIMHA SWAMI, B.V. *Self-realization: Life & Teachings of Shri Ramana Maharshi.* 7th edition. Tiruvannamalai: Sri Ramanasramam, 1968

RICE, Edward. *Eastern Definitions.* New York: Doubleday, 1978

TAGORE, Rabindranath. *Fireflies.* New York: Macmillan, 1966

The ten principal Upanishads, put into English by Shree Purohit Swami and W.B. Yeats. London: Faber and Faber, 1937

Upanishads; edited by K.P. Bahadur. New Delhi: Heritage Publishers, 1979

WALKER, Benjamin. *Hindu World.* London: George Allen & Unwin, 1968

II
JAINISM

Of the four main Indian religions discussed in this book, Jainism remains the only one that failed to be popularly known beyond the frontiers of India. The rigorous self-denial expected of its adherents may well have been an important reason of its failure to become a widely popular religious movement. Even within India the Jains today constitute only an estimated three millions. However, they are a socially powerful and influential community on account of their material prosperity.

So ancient is Jainism that sometimes it is claimed to be the primordial religion of India, even older than Hinduism itself! Over the centuries it has influenced, and been influenced by, both Hindu and Buddhist thought. Jainism and Buddhism, which are both basically atheistic, were two of the important 'heresies' that challenged the ideas and beliefs of Brahmanism.

Etymologically, the word 'Jain' is derived from the Sanskrit *ji* (to conquer) and hence *jina* (conqueror). For the sole purpose of the Jain's spiritual struggle is to free the soul from its imprisoned state in matter so that it knows the bliss of immortality. Their religious endeavours are designed to culminate in this highest of all conquests.

According to Jain tradition, the timeless truths enshrined in their religion were given utterance by a long line of twenty-four *jinas* or 'conquerors', also called Tirthankaras.

Rishabha was the first of the Tirthankaras but little is known about his life. He had, like Mahāvira later, practised austerities of an extreme kind before becom ing a preacher of wisdom. Whereas our informatior about the first twenty-two Tirthankaras remains shrouded in the mists of unrecorded history; the last two *jinas*, however, are regarded as having been historical personalities. The predecessor of Mahāvira was Pārsva, the twenty-third *jina*, who lived about 817 B.C. Mahāvira, the twenty-fourth Tirthankara, was the last exponent of this ancient teaching, and therefore he should not strictly be called the 'founder of Jainism', as is popularly done.

The quietness, tidiness and cleanliness of Jain temples in India are features that have always impressed me. They are sanctuaries of peace and refuge from the squalor, dust and noise of crowded Indian cities. The centres of interest in these temples are naturally the white alabaster statues of the twenty-four Tirthankaras, usually arranged in a row. Devotees worship these statues, beginning with the last or twenty-fourth Tirthankara and ending with the first, by anointing them with coloured liquids and offering flowers. As the various Tirthankaras were not celestial beings but only humans who liberated themselves, it is odd that they are worshipped as though they were gods. Actually any kind of worship must violate the Jain principle of absolute self-reliance in the attainment of enlightenment which means that every person should be his own saviour, for there is no such thing or person called God who is capable of helping. Jains reject the Hindu belief in a God, who is regarded as the creator, sustainer and destroyer of the universe. God is a mere fictitious concept and not a concrete reality. It is to the credit of the *digambara* school of Jains that they refuse to participate in temple worship or idolatry.

The life of Mahāvira (*circa 540-468 B.C.*)

Mahāvira, which means "The Great Hero', is also called the *jina* or 'The Conqueror'. Whereas it is comparatively easy to conquer a kingdom, subjugate an alien race or seize others' mundane possessions; it is infinitely more difficult to become a master of spirituality. Only that kind of rare person, who transcends his psychological limitations and casts aside his egoistic and animalistic nature, deserves to be called 'Conqueror'. Jains believe that Mahāvira was such a person.

He was a senior contemporary of the Buddha and in the Buddhist scriptures has been regarded as one of his main antagonists.

Prince Vardhamāna, known later as Mahāvira, was born as the second son into a royal family for his parents were King Siddhārtha, chief of the Jnatrika clan, and Queen Trishalā. It is said that after he was conceived in his mother's womb, she had seen fourteen great dreams which, according to the Jain scriptures, indicated beforehand that the child was going to become either an emperor or a Tirthankara, a person who attains *nirvana* or *moksha*, which is the state of spiritual perfection. He was born at Kundagrāma in the Indian state of Bihar into the Kshatriya or warrior-ruler caste. The Buddha also was born into this caste, which at that time was politically powerful.

Little is known about his boyhood. He underwent the training of a warrior. As he was reared in an environment of princely riches, this period of his life was presumably a happy one. He is described as having been an unusually handsome boy, strong, fearless and highly intelligent. There is a story of a big snake entering the garden where he was playing. His fear-stricken companion fled, but Vardhamāna courageously caught hold of the dangerous serpent and flung it away.

His marriage to Yasodā, a noblewoman, resulted in the birth of a daughter. This daughter got married to Jamali, who after the death of Mahāvira became the first dissenter in the history of Jainism. Some believe that Vardhamāna had two children. The *Digambara* Jains however insist that he never married but remained a lifelong celibate.

Vardhamāna's mind was conditioned by Jain religious ideals and ethical values during his childhood, youth and manhood since his parents were followers of Pārsva, the twenty-third Thirthankara, who is believed to have lived about two centuries before him. His father and mother must have been strict devotees because they ended their lives by voluntary starvation, as required by their creed. The followers of Pārsva were called *nirgranthas* ('Free from Bonds'), and this term was later used to refer to those belonging to the order started by Mahāvira.

His parents died when he was twenty-eight, whereupon he wanted to renounce the world immediately. In all likelihood this blow caused him so much distress that it turned his mind to spiritual interests. But his elder brother, who succeeded to the principality, prevailed upon him to stay at home. He agreed to remain involved in family life for just another two years. These two years of self-discipline foreshadowed the years of austerity which were to follow. For he gave up dressing his hair, wearing garlands of flowers as well as using articles of luxury. He also gave generous alms to beggars during this period.

Around the age of thirty, having obtained the permission of his elder brother, he renounced the world by disposing of his wealth, abandoning all worldly pleasures and leaving his wife, family and relatives.

The Great Renunciation took place in the presence of his relatives and other people. He was carried from his home in a palanquin to a garden where, under the shade of an asoka tree, he reduced himself to the humble state of nakedness by removing all his ornaments and clothes. He plucked out the hair from his head and body in five handfuls and threw it away and then put a single holy cloth on his shoulder. On a later occasion he gave away half of it to a Brahmin beggar. The other half remained on his shoulder for thirteen months until it was ripped off by a thorny shrub during his wanderings. Since that time he remained totally naked.

In one version of the Great Renunciation he is reported to have solemnly uttered these words:

> "I bow down to all the liberated souls."

Thereupon he took the five vows of non-violence, devotion to truth, non-stealing, celibacy and non-possession, in the expectation of destroying all past Karma and not accumulating any fresh Karma henceforth.

In another version of the Great Renunciation it is said that the following vow was taken by him:

> "From now until my death I will observe equality towards all creatures; I will not sin with my mind, speech or body; I will not get another to sin for me nor approve of sinning by others; I am repentant of all the sins committed by me in the past and I will refrain from them in the future."

When he initiated himself thus he was conforming to the age-old practice of self-initiation by previous Tirthankaras. This practice underlines an important principle of both Jain and Buddhist philosophy — the principle of total self-dependence in spiritual matters.

Vardhamāna began his period of *sādhanā* (spiritual

apprenticeship) by resolving that he would not take care of his body for twelve years and that he would silently endure all obstacles and suffering as well as forgiving those who persecuted him.

For twelve long years he wandered over the Gangetic plain and meditated and practised self-mortification. He was a true homeless wanderer in the sense that during this time he never stayed for more than a single night in a village nor five nights in a town, only when the rainy season came he spent about four months in one place.

In his quest for Truth, Gautama, the Buddha-to-be, went from teacher to teacher but became dissatisfied with all of them. Vardhamāna, however, evidently did not have to undertake such a course of searching because he was already deeply committed to the teachings of Pārsva, the twenty-third Tirthankara. Therefore he had to concern himself only with ridding his soul of the ties of Karma through intense asceticism.

It is believed that because he did not make the common mistake of identifying his soul with the body, but was immersed in the soul instead, he remained unaffected by every kind of bodily pain. Physical discomforts ceased to bother him. His unclothed body was always exposed to the elements, but his inner tranquillity remained undisturbed at all times, regardless of whether he meditated under the scorching sun or in extremities of cold.

As he walked he carefully watched the path before him lest any poor living creature was trodden underfoot. He preferred to stay in solitary places such as abandoned houses or cemeteries. The meagre food he needed to keep himself alive was obtained by begging.

Although differentiating fact from fiction is a well-known difficulty in all religious literature, it is nevertheless interesting to note the legends that have been woven around the lives of religious leaders, because millions believe that such things actually happened and these beliefs condition their outlook. It was said that a certain monk had died in a fit of anger and consequently been reborn as a very dangerous and venomous serpent which could reduce anyone to ashes by its mere glance. People were unsuccessful in dissuading Vardhamāna from going to see that serpent. He approached the mouth of the pit where it lived and meditated deeply. Thereupon the angry serpent rushed out but failed to burn him. The serpent then bit his feet thrice but was surprised that Vardhamāna remained calm and undisturbed. Vardhamana said:

> "O Chanda Kaushika, be enlightened and attain peace of mind."

The words 'Chanda Kaushika' rekindled buried memories in the serpent, which remembered its misdeeds committed in bygone lives. Vardhamāna gave it spiritual precepts and the repentant serpent eschewed its violent tendencies once and for all. A few days later the serpent died peacefully and was reborn in a celestial abode.

There came a period in Vardhamāna's life when he fasted for varying lengths of time in the course of practising austerities. It is stated that the god Samgamaka inflicted severe physical pain on Vardhamāna, he remained tranquil and unmoved. The god next started accompanying Vardhamāna on his begging rounds and contaminating the food that was offered him. He naturally stopped asking for alms. When the god realized that harassing him was of no avail, he begged to be forgiven and left. It was then that Vardhamāna ended the fast that had lasted six months.

The Jain scriptures refer to the gods who tortured Vardhamāna with the malicious intention of turning his mind away from austerities and rigorous self-discipline. One wonders whether these accounts of mischievous activities by gods are not meant to be purely allegorical. Are these gods merely symbolic of various evil forces, like desires or temptations which suddenly appear and thereby test the progress or otherwise of the spiritual aspirant?

It is said that on one occasion certain government officials tried to execute Vardhamāna whom they regarded as a robber. But he refused to reveal his identity. When they tried to kill him by hanging, the rope snapped seven times in succession. Realizing that their efforts were fruitless, they decided to release him.

An extremely difficult vow to fulfil, because of the many conditions attached to it, was called *abhigraha*. In the twelfth year of his initiation Vardhamāna vowed that the fast he began at Kaushambi would be terminated only with his acceptance of alms from a donor who fulfilled his ten untold conditions: He would accept boiled pulse from the corner of a winnowing basket, offered by a person with one leg on the threshold and the other outside, who though a slave now was once a princess, whose head was shaven and whose legs were in fetters. Furthermore, she must be a chaste person having performed three days' fasting; she should make the offering to him after all mendicants had left and also with tears in her eyes. He was determined to continue fasting unless the donor fulfilled all these preconditions. Vardhamāna walked the streets of Kaushambi every day but failed to receive alms under the conditions he had stipulated. For a period of five months and twenty days he lived without taking any food until there was a donor who satisfied all these detailed conditions except one. She was Princess Chandanā, then living as a slave girl, who happened to be shackled and shaved by a rich merchant's jealous wife.

When Chandanā offered him alms, Vardhamāna turned away from her without accepting it. This gesture of his made her cry. There were tears in her eyes and so the last condition of his vow was met. The food was then accepted and the long fast was broken.

Once Vardhamāna was meditating near a certain village when a cowherd left his oxen near him and asked him to watch the animals while he was away. But when he returned the cattle were missing. He persistently questioned Vardhamāna about the missing animals but he remained silent. The cowherd got so angry that he inserted wooden pegs into his ears but he patiently tolerated the pain. Later these pegs were extracted by an eminent physician by using pincers. It is reported that the pain was so agonising that it made him cry out.

Because of his great capacity to bear pain, privation and even persecution uncomplainingly, Vadhamāna rightly deserves to be called 'Mahāvira' or the 'Great Hero', although the strict application of that title belongs to the period only after, and not before, his attainment of *Nirvana*.

Twelve long years of preparatory self-purification had passed. It was in the thirteenth year of his spiritual quest that the long-awaited spiritual summit was reached. The great awakening happened under a sāla tree by the bank of the river Rijuvālukā. In a squatting position ('cow-milking posture') he was meditating profoundly, while in the state of a two-day fast during which period not even water was drunk, when he attained the state of absolute knowledge or *kevalajnāna* or *nirvana*. In the words of the *Kalpasutra*:

> "Then the Shramana Lord Mahāvira became an *arhat*, *jina*, *kevali*, all-knowing and all-seeing . . . ."

Jains believe that he became omniscient, comprehending everything in the entire universe, including everything in the past, present and future.

It is significant that Mahāvira departed from the tradition of preaching in Sanskrit and gave preference to a popular dialect called Ardhamāgadhi, probably because he wanted his message conveyed to a wider audience, and especially to the common people instead of confining it to the learned classes.

Numerous indeed were the persons who got converted after listening to Mahāvira's discourses as he travelled from place to place for thirty years, after the attainment of absolute knowledge or *kevalajnāna*. There was, for instance, the famous Brahmin scholar, Indrabhuti Gautama, who wanted to challenge Mahāvira and defeat him in argument. But he was so overwhelmed by the personality and teachings of Mahāvira that he, along with his five hundred disciples, got initiated into the new religion. It should be mentioned that many disciples of the twenty-third Tirthankara, Pārsva, also became followers of Mahāvira once they realized that Mahāvira *was* no other than the twenty-fourth Tirthankara and hence worthy of reverence. Prospective disciples usually questioned him on controversial doctrinal matters and accepted his spiritual leadership only after they were fully satisfied with his answers. His disciples included Vedic scholars, ascetics, itinerant monks and persons from different orders and callings. It is interesting that although Mahāvira and the Buddha were considered as rivals, they both enjoyed the patronage of the very same kings. As he became increasingly well-known for his saintliness and wisdom, more and more disciples joined him with the result that at one time he had an estimated fourteen-thousand followers.

He spent the last rainy season of his life in the village of Pāwā. There at the age of seventy two, he died one morning while in the midst of delivering a sermon. In the words of the *Kalpasutra*:

> "Lord Mahāvira, the great *Shramana*, breathed his last, passed away from this world, departed above, never to return again. Casting aside the chains of birth, decrepitude and death, he became self-fulfilled, enlightened and liberated, rid of all *karma*, secure in the ultimate emancipation and immune to all suffering."

Some of the chieftains present at his death believed that the light of knowledge, indeed the Light of the world. had been extinguished. So they lit candles, thus originated the Jain testival of lights or Dev Divali in commemoration of this event, which is celebrated on the tenth day after the Hindu Divali.

The Jain Theory of Karma

It is necessary to reiterate that Jainism is emphatically atheistic. It denies the existence of an Absolute with which all creation should eventually become united or merged. There is instead a dualistic system according to which the cosmos has its spirit but man too has his own immortal spirit, quite independent of that of the cosmos. Indeed every atom of earth, fire, water and wind, including every plant and animal has its own eternal spirit or soul. If may be noted that throughout this chapter the word 'spirit' is used as synonymous with the word 'soul' Jains adhere to the animistic view that souls are present in all things.

The soul goes on reincarnating itself endlessly until it finds the peace of Liberation, when this painful process of births and deaths comes to an end. It is the accumulated past deeds and desires that keep the soul in bondage. It is Karma, in other words, that keeps us in servitude; it is the state of *karmalessness* that will ensure that much sought final release of the spirit — *nirvana*.

The Jain theory of Karma is most interesting because Karma is regarded as a form of impure matter that gets attached to the pure soul with the result that the latter is reduced to a state of subjugation. Freedom cannot be won unless the soul is divested of this *Karmic* matter through an arduous process of practising austerities. Karma may be likened to the worthless, husk-like and earthen accretion that has enveloped a precious diamond. Without the removal of Karma the soul will never experience the non-reincarnating state of eternal bliss.

This subtle and invisible matter of Karma gets attached to the soul and it is this amalgam that causes the soul to migrate miserably from one life to another. Depending on whether one's store of Karma happens to be favourable or otherwise, one is reborn into a pleasant or unpleasant state respectively. One has to reap the fruits of past deeds in the form of Karma, and only when the effects of Karma have been fully discharged is the soul free again. This process of purgation or purification, called *nirjarā*, if extended to the entire range of one's accumulated Karma, results in the emancipation of the soul.

According to the dualistic philosophy of Jainism, the contents of the universe are either *jiva* (conscious) or *ajiva* (unconscious). The immortal and non-material souls or the *jivas* are to be found not only within man but in all living matter. Souls are indestructible and never lose their identity by, say, merging into any divine entity. The *ajiva* or non-conscious part of the universe is comprised of matter of various sorts. In contrast, the *jiva*, the spirit or the soul, has the qualities of intelligence, peace, power and faith. But these desirable qualities of the soul disappear, when the *jiva* itself is enmeshed in the materialistic web of Karma. The problem, then, is to strip the *jiva* of the undesirable *ajiva* elements that have got attached to it. The soul, in other words, has to be thoroughly cleansed of its *karmic* matter.

This theory is based on the assumption that matter and spirit can co-exist. The questions that arise are: If spirit were so pure, why did it ever get joined to matter and get contaminated? And is spirit at all susceptible to such pollution and corruption? If the soul were so inherently pure, how can it ever get defiled? One should have thought that the two streams of matter and spirit were quite distinct and mutually exclusive, with the result that any association between them is quite out of the question.

It is difficult to reconcile the contradiction that is contained in this theory. But when a theory rests on mere belief, why expect it to have a rational foundation?

When one is cleansed of Karma, there is a flowering of the *triratna* ('Three Jewels') or three excellences of right faith, right knowledge and right conduct, which are the prerequisites for the attainment of *nirvana*.

The destiny of the soul that is totally freed from its *karmic* fetters is described in the *Uttarādhyayana Sutra* (Book of Later Instructions):

> "Taking the form of a straight line, the soul moves in a single movement without touching anything, travels upward and there grows into its natural form, obtains Perfection, Enlightenment, Deliverance and Ultimate Beatitude and all suffering is ended."

It is believed that liberated souls travel to the top of the universe, above the highest heaven, where they remain eternally in a state of omniscient bliss. Incidentally, if the universe were infinitely vast in all directions, can it have either a 'top' or a 'bottom'?

Jains maintain that the liberation of the soul can take place only when one is born as a human being. So rare and difficult and precious is such a birth that the opportunity of finding salvation should not be missed by us. In the *Sutrakritanga Sutra* Mahāvira pointed out that every effort should be made to attain true knowledge before it was too late. For the time past can never return and death may come at any time. Consequently the lives of serious minded Jains, including that of Mahāvira himself, have always been characterised by a sense of urgency and a burning zealousness.

Supreme Importance of Non-Injury (*ahimsa*)

Jainism emphasizes the importance of the sanctity of life far more than any other Indian religion. Jains hold that any kind of killing, intentional or otherwise, makes the weight of Karma particularly burdensome.

The *Jaina Sutras* declare:

> "People are wicked who kill living beings for their own pleasure."
>
> "He who lights a fire, kills living beings; he who extinguishes the fire, kills the fire. Therefore a wise man who respects the Law must light no fire."
>
> "Earth and water contains life; jumping insects as well as dirtborn vermin get burned when a fire is lit."
>
> "Sprouts are beings that develop and have their own individual lives. By cutting them down for

> pleasure many living beings get destroyed. By destroying seeds that are young or mature a careless man harms his own soul."
>
> "People are wicked when they destroy seeds for the purpose of their own pleasure."

Jain literature abounds in references to *ahimsa*, such as the *Uttarādhyayana Sutra* which states that the essence of the wisdom of a wise man consists in not hurting any creature: he is equal minded to all creatures and regards them as his own self.

Ahimsa is the *foremost* vow that is observed by all Jains. They go to the extreme length of not participating in certain occupations such as agriculture as it entails the killing of insects that thrive in the soil. Consequently many Jains engage themselves in occupations such as money-lending or commerce. Many of them have succeeded in amassing vast fortunes in a country of such abject poverty.

There are certain questions that wealthy Jains could be asked. Are your ostentatious acts of charity sincerely intended to alleviate poverty? Are these acts not frequently motivated solely by the desire to acquire merit for yourself, which, incidentally, is just an expression of the same self-centred greed which craves for position, power and money? Why confine the application of the doctrine of *ahimsa* to non-killing only, when it ought to include also the avoidance of pain and hardship caused by the economic exploitation of the financially weak by the financially strong? Does not the accumulation of riches amount to a kind of injury that is inflicted on those classes whose lot is extreme poverty? Is not the lack of interest in sharing *substantial* portions of your income with the poor, a sign of callous indifference to their suffering? Is not neglecting to feed the starving a kind of indirect killing?

On account of the belief that life is manifest in every living atom, Jains strive never to injure, let alone kill, any form of life. They are haunted by the fear that injuring and killing will only increase, and never decrease, their Karma. Therefore some Jains wear before their noses and mouths pieces of gauze so that no living creature is inadvertently drawn into their lungs when inhaling. It is not realized, however, that every time a person inhales air or drinks water, some of the microscopic organisms that unavoidably enter into his body get destroyed, and no gauze can possibly prevent that from happening.

In order to avoid even the accidental and unintentional killing of a living being, a monk must be very careful and watchful when walking, talking and begging for food. When walking a monk should look at the ground ahead of him for about six feet, lest he tramples upon any living being. He must inspect and sweep the ground before he places anything upon it lest he injures or destroys any form of life. Therefore monks carry brooms when they walk, in order to sweep the path to the right and left before them so that no living creature is accidentally trodden. But Digambaras use peacocks' feathers instead of brooms for this purpose. Every time one goes for a walk there is the risk of trampling upon and crushing to death invisible forms of life. Is sweeping an effective safeguard against that kind of killing?

On seeing Jain monks in India with their faces half covered with gauzes and carrying brooms or peacocks' feathers, I have often wondered whether these persons were not making a public display of their piety. Is there not an element of vanity and a certain lack of humility when monks parade their supposed religiosity?

Sterilization and disinfection, which are important means of controlling the spread of diseases, necessarily involve the killing of numerous forms of life. Our good health depends largely on how successfully we eliminate pests and vermin that threaten our very existence.

That life depends on life is an easily observable phenomenon. In the oceans, for example, the tiny fish are eaten by the large fish who in turn are eaten by the even larger kinds of fish. Even vegetarians are not entirely blameless because the nuts, fruits and vegetables that they consume are also forms of life. Remembering the belief that every atom is pervaded by life, the Jain doctrine of *ahimsa* cannot be fully and faithfully observed, unless one totally gives up not only eating and drinking but breathing as well. It would seem that the only logical course open to the truly devout Jain is to opt to die!

In view of the fact that the destruction of life is regrettably inevitable in the course of everyday living, one wishes the Jain scriptures had recognized this difficulty, and then, in the light of this understanding, enjoined the Jains to avoid such destruction only within the bounds of reasonable possibility. No moral code should become so lofty as to lose touch with the hard surface of reality. When followers realize the utter impracticability of certain rules, will not their sense of failure and attendant guilt feelings tend to increase and worsen?

One can injure and kill either intentionally of unintentionally (i.e. accidentally): Jain householders are expected to refrain from the former totally and from the latter as much as possible. Because householders would find it almost impossible to do their domestic chores on account of the rule against the destruction of any living thing, they would only be expected to avoid intentional killing. Does this mean that they would be absolved from the Karma resulting from killing that happens unwittingly?

A monk is expected to lead a lite of extreme self-restraint, in the course of which he should overcome twenty-two things that have the propensity to trouble and distract him. This list includes overcoming the sense of dissatisfaction, hunger, thirst, cold, heat and the distress caused by mosquitoes and gnats; and also the feeling of shame caused by one's own nudity for monks should not wear any clothes.

If at the end of twelve years a monk succeeds in observing all the prescribed rules of religious conduct, he is allowed the spiritual honour of starving himself to death (which is regarded as the highest and noblest austerity) so that his soul, now released from the bonds of Karma, enters into the state of immortality. It would seem that for a monk life has no purpose other than that of self-purification, leading to self-inflicted death, which is the prelude to the soul's perpetual state of deathlessness.

Voluntary religious death via self-starvation is practised by both Jain monks and pious laymen, either as the holiest culmination of their religious lives or during an emergency, such as when death is imminent or when suffering from a terminal illness. Pious laymen engage themselves in self-mortification for a period of twelve months, instead of the required period of twelve years for monks, before taking their own lives. If a monk finds that he cannot live up to the rules, he must choose to die instead of violating them. During his period of self-mortification he must, however, try to avoid dying prematurely because his highest goal should be the removal of every stain of Karma that blemishes his otherwise pure soul.

We have already seen how the monk who succeeds in observing his vows must take the ultimate step of intentionally ending his own life. Let us honestly admit that the term 'voluntary death' is just a religious euphemism fo. what is ordinarily called 'suicide', but Jains strongly object to the word 'suicide'. Is not suicide a kind of violence that is directed against oneself? When that violence results in the death of another, it is called homicide, but when it causes one's own demise it is termed suicide: in both cases the instinct to injure and kill is not only present but is given ample expression. Is it not very strange that suicide is condoned and even elevated to the status of a great virtue in a religion that extols non-injury or *ahimsa*? Besides, do monks who are going to kill themselves ever consider the consequent grief of their relatives, friends and other loved ones? And once the body is dead, will not the organisms that lived within it, also have to face eventual death for the lack of nourishment?

Orthodox Jains are vegans in the sense that they live solely on the products of the plant kingdom and exclude from their diet foods such as flesh, fish, fowl, eggs, even animal milk and its derivatives as well as honey. Also there are cetain kinds of vegetables and fruits that are avoided. For instance, they are forbidden to take vegetables and roots that are bulbous in shape with stalks, such as mushrooms, onions and aubergines. Orthodox Jains minutely examine fruits and vegetables before eating them to ensure that they are entirely free of insects. For the same reason they carefully strain water before using it. Strict Jains prefer to take their meals before sunset because insects appear after it is dark.

Needless to say, the sacrificing of animals as practised by some Hindu sects to appease certain bloodthirsty gods, is a strange 'religious' practice that is particularly abhorrent to Jains. Indeed they even strongly object to the sacrificing of an artificial image of an animal since such a deed involves the thought or intention of destroying life.

Actually *ahimsa* should not be seen merely as a philosophy of negative action, for it also requires involvement in positive acts of loving kindness. Harmless conduct needs to be supplemented with good deeds that spring from the depths of compassion. True *ahimsa* must originate in altruistic benevolence. Therefore, tender hearted Jains care for the welfare of all animals and humans. The feeding of ants, for instance, is a popular practice among the Jains.

It is highly commendable that Jains maintain institutions where old and sick animals and birds are looked after until the end of their days. Nevertheless, a question that should be asked is whether this 'caring' for animals is motivated by a sense of religious duty, or is the natural flowering of real concern and loving kindness? Are these poor animals well treated because they are seen as being important in themselves, or merely because such 'kind' acts are intended to diminish Karma? Surely animals deserve to be lovingly tended for their own sake, rather than *used* as a means to promote one's own spiritual advancement.

The Jain doctrine of *ahimsa* influenced the attitudes and thinking of Mahatma Gandhi, the greatest exponent of non-violence in recent times. This teaching of eschewing violence is indeed particularly suitable for a world like ours which is so deeply committed to militarism.

The Purity of Nudity

Towards the end of the reign of Emperor Chandragupta (circa 317 - 293 B.C), the Jain community was split by a major schism. When Bhadrabāhu, the Jain leader and Gandhara realized that there was going to be a major famine in North India, he advised the Jains to migrate to South India. He did not succeed in persuading all, but a large group, including the Emperor Chandragupta, joined him and they moved to the Deccan plateau in the south. When they returned home twenty years later, it was noticed that the northern group had gone astray because they had adopted the questionable practice of wearing clothes. Owing to the hardships caused by the famine, Sthūlabhadra, the leader of the monks, had permitted the wearing of white garments.

Of the various dissensions that divided the Jains probably the most notable one centred around the question of whether it is proper for Jains to be clad or unclad. The Svetāmbara ('white clad') school argued for the wearing of clothes. But the Digambara ('sky clad') school renounced all clothing.

Clothes are a symbol of man's sense of advancement in society, whereas nudity is only natural for a person who renounces all, including the self. The ego's sense of importance and respectability is sustained by the clothes we wear. Dress is often a form of vanity because these stitched pieces of cloth that we wear help mainly to conceal our essential and inherent nakedness which we shun facing. Clothes are masks with which we conveniently disguise our real selves. No baby was ever born clothed. The discarding of apparel is a step towards restoring that lost primordial innocence and purity.

Groups of naked Digambara monks uninhibitedly travel around India, a country warm enough for nudism to be comfortably practised, and their presence is especially conspicuous at religious festivals.

The Digambaras and Svetāmbaras have many doctrines in common despite their differences. Their main disagreement was caused only by the insistence of the Digambaras on the absolute necessity of nudity, at least for the monks.

It is reported that Bhadrabāhu fasted and did penance in solitude in the Himalayas because he was so disturbed by this aforementioned schism. His withdrawal was a great loss because he was the last person to know perfectly the unwritten doctrines of the Jains. When he died, Sthūlabhadra summoned a general council at Patna with the intention of reconstructing the doctrines, based on what the monks remembered. They succeeded in producing only a partial canon, known as the twelve *angas* ('Limbs') or sections. The Digambaras question the authenticity of the *angas* which are accepted only by the Svetāmbaras. The discontented Digambaras prepared new scriptures for themselves.

One should have thought that the Digambaras, a sect that feels itself so liberated, would regard women with a liberal attitude. Unfortunately, however, the Digambaras maintain that women cannot attain salvation and hence they are debarred from monastic life. The Svetāmbaras argue that the nineteenth Tirthankara, Malli, was a woman but the Digambaras deny this claim. If every living being has a soul, which must sooner or later attain immortality, why then treat women as though they were devoid of souls? Their prejudice against women cannot be justified.

The Path of Austerity

The sole aim of practising *tapas* or austerities is to extinguish all old Karma. The strict ethical system of the Jains has been inspired by the need to free their souls from the enslaving effects of Karma. They aspire not only to rid themselves of all old Karma but also to prevent the influx of new Karma.

The fourfold community of Jains (*samgha*) that was founded by Mahāvira consists of monks, nuns, laymen and laywomen.

On joining their Order, Jain monks commit themselves to the strict observance of the five great vows. They vow to abstain from killing, lying, stealing and sexual intercourse as well as to renounce all worldly possessions. No monk can be seriously faithful to the last of these vows unless he reduces himself to a state of utter poverty and mendicancy.

Laymen and laywomen adhere to the requirements of these vows but less strictly than the monks: the rules of discipline that are practised do not differ in kind but only in their degree of application. Both monks and householders, in other words, have more or less the same religious duties to perform, but the former are understandably expected to dedicate themselves to these obligations with greater intensity than the latter.

For a limited period a layman is at liberty to take a vow from the following category of vows, which are less exacting than those taken by monks: limiting the distances up to which he will go in any given direction; abstaining from involvement in matters that do not really concern him; limiting his food, drink and other enjoyments, and living as a monk on certain specified days. Some laymen may never wish to become monks, but they hope, nevertheless, that they would at least derive some of the benefits of renunciation by temporarily taking these vows.

We have already referred to the five great vows that are taken by monks. Let us now consider some of the detailed and supplementary rules that have to be followed by them.

Monks shave their heads but it is preferred that they remove their hair by the painful process of plucking it out as Mahāvira did when he renounced the world. The utter simplicity of a monk is such that his few possessions are confined to an almsbowl, a stick, a broom or peacocks' feathers for sweeping the ground, a gauze to cover his mouth and ward off insects, a blanket and some clothes (except for the naked Digambaras).

Does real simplicity consist in having a few materia belongings, or rather in that state when the mind is free of all psychological wants? A monk may ostentatiously embrace poverty, but if he were trying to acquire various virtues, and is driven by various desires, even the desire for spiritual betterment, is he acting in the true spirit of the Jain canon? Is a mind that is entrapped in the processes of achieving, striving and struggling actually in a state of tranquillity or simplicity?

Monks are expected to deliver sermons and explain their Jain sacred writings to the laity, which they usually do in the *upāsrayas* or special buildings where they reside from time to time.

A monk is required to cultivate only good thoughts. Does this practice not amount to a kind of repression which is the cause of many a neurosis? A mind that encourages the emergence of 'good' thoughts and shuns 'bad' thoughts is soon reduced to a battlefield of conflict. An 'undesirable' thought violently brushed aside is never permanently ousted from the field of consciousness, but continues to lurk in some hidden corner of the mind. It is far wiser to allow such a thought to remain uninterfered so that it can surface. Then it can be fully faced, understood and hence dissolved. This process of emptying the mind of its hidden conflicts and complexes is real meditation. But the cultivation of good' thoughts, which necessarily involves the avoidance of 'bad' thoughts, is a futile practice that results in the accumulation of defilements within the mind, which is the very opposite of purification. This criticism can be levelled against all ethical codes and systems of meditation that involve any tampering with the free flow of the thought process, and especially the Jain monk's strict code of conduct. For he must eschew vices such as anger, pride and greed and cultivate virtues like forbearance, purity, poverty and chastity.

A monk's outlook is so heavily conditioned by a pessimistic and gloomy view of life that he is naturally constrained to contemplate such matters as the transitoriness of all things and the unhappiness of the world. Now, is it factually correct that life is totally devoid of happiness? If the monks experience unhappiness, surely one of the important contributory factors is their general indifference to beauty. There is a great joy in the appreciation of beauty but this joy cannot be experienced by those who regard beautiful sights as 'sinful sensory experiences'. Only a person who has deliberately made himself utterly insensitive can remain unmoved by the sight of an enchanting scene or the multicoloured sky at sunset. Their unhappiness gets aggravated because they must uncomplainingly tolerate various ordeals and physical discomforts such as thirst, cold, heat and illness.

Jainism is hardly the religion for anyone who seeks physical gratification or psychological consolation, as people in general do, for its strict spiritual exercises and various painful practices are very trying and border on the tortuous. This fact becomes particularly evident when one considers the Jain forms of *tapas*.

Apart from the question of fasting until death which has already been considered, less rigorous fasting is an austerity greatly favoured. A popular form of fasting is eating only once every second, third, fourth, fifth day, etc. until the limit of once every six months is reached. Neither should monks eat food that has been specially made for them nor partake of food that is tasty or attractive. Thus, among other things, they should deny themselves the pleasures of the palate also.

A monk who commits a serious sin has to confess it

to a superior who may prescribe various penances. He may have to be ordained again, if he were guilty of a serious transgression.

Does Asceticism Weaken or Strengthen the Self?

A concept that is basic to Jainism is that it is only through self-mortification that *moksha* can be realized. Penitential discipline is seen as the only means of finding salvation. This assumption should be examined and not taken for gospel.

What satisfactions do monks, Yogis and others derive from self-punishment and self-control? Besides, what is the agency that is trying to control desires? There is no point in practising self-control unless one asks this fundamental question: who is the *controller* practising self-control? It will be seen that the controller is no other than the 'I' or 'ego', that illusory sense of personality. Any exercise of will must necessarily emanate from the ego. Will does not spring from nowhere. Will is the creation of the ego. Through will the ego expresses itself. The restless ego ceaselessly asserts itself in order to keep itself strong, active and alive. Self-mortification is admittedly painful but it is tolerated because there is the hope of achieving self-mastery after a long struggle. The feeling that one has succeeded in conquering one's instincts and subjugated various undesirable tendencies gives the ego a tremendous sense of power, importance and prestige. What is the good of asceticism, if it were going to fortify the ego instead of eliminating it altogether? Moreover, is the controller basically different from that which is controlled? Suppose a monk tries to eradicate, let us say, ambition from his mind, as he has come to regard it as a great obstacle to spiritual progress. Is the entity that is fighting ambition with the intention of destroying it, not itself part and parcel of ambition itself? The ambitious ego deceptively attempts to cast aside ambition as though it were itself free of ambition! Similarly, the ego tries to cleanse itself of lust, not realizing that it is itself the abode of lust. Since the ego is nothing but a conglomeration of our psychological traits, is there any sense in using the will of the self as an instrument for self-purification?

It is a tribute to the extraordinary intelligence of Gautama The Buddha that it did not take him very long to realize the limitations inherent in the timeworn practice of 'spiritual' masochism, which is variously described as self-mortification, self-punishment and self-torture. After having experimented with asceticism for awhile, he had the clarity of mind to abandon it altogether, which decision, in a sense, precipitated his attainment of Buddhahood. Could it be that Mahāvira, too, achieved *nirvana* but not because of his having practised austerities, but despite them?

What is Real Renunciation?

It is reported in the *Dasavaikālika Sutra* that mere physical possession was not regarded as possession by Mahāvira. For it is *attachment* that constitutes possession. In the light of this statement, it would seem that a monk who 'renounces' the world, and 'gives up' all his belongings, is not necessarily a person without possessions, so long as he has attachments for them. On the other hand, an individual who lives in an opulent palace, surrounded by beautiful objets d'art, could well be really renunciative, provided he is psychologically free of all attachments. So it is the inward state of the mind that indicates whether one has truly renounced or otherwise.

The nature of renunciation is explained in the *Āchārānga Sutra*. One cannot possibly stop what is experienced by the various sense organs — the sounds that enter the ears, the forms that pass before the eyes, the smells that enter the nose, the taste that is felt upon the palate and the objects that touch the body. Nevertheless, one should neither be attracted nor repulsed by these experiences.

So long as the body is alive, alert and healthy, it will continue to have experiences via these sense organs. The flow of experiences via the senses cannot be checked; there is nothing to be gained by trying to check them. What one can do, however, is to remain so awake that one is detached vis-à-vis these experiences. And it is not at all necessary to become a recluse and retire into a forest to possess constantly that inner quality of detachment. Is it not possible to remain pure and unspoilt, while earning one's livelihood, in an impure society? Is it not possible to live in a world that is acquisitive, violent and ruthless and still be utterly detached from the ways of the world?

SELECT BIBLIOGRAPHY

BASHAM, A.L. *The Wonder That Was India*. New and revised edition. New York : Hawthorn Books, 1963

Encyclopaedia of Religion and Ethics; edited by James Hastings. Edinburgh: T. & T. Clark, 1959

GRANT, Francis. *Oriental Philosophy*. New York: Dial Press, 1938

PANDEY, B.N. *A Book of India*. London: Collins, 1965

RADHAKRISHNAN, S. *Indian Religions*. New Delhi: Vision Books, 1979

RICE, Edward. *Eastern Definitions*. New York: Doubleday, 1978

SAMSOOKHA, Puranchand. *Lord Mahāvira (His Life & Doctrines)*. 2nd edition. Calcutta: Jain Swetambar Terapanthi Mahasabha, 1957

SPEAR, Percival. *India: A Modern History*. Ann Arbor: University of Michigan Press, 1961

SPIEGELBERG, Frederic. *Living Religions of the World*. London: Thames and Husdon, 1957

THOMAS, P. *Festivals and Holidays of India*. Bombay: D.B. Taraporevala, 1971

UPADHYE, A.N. *Jainism* (In *A Cultural History of India;* edited by A.L. Basham. Delhi: Oxford University Press, 1983)

WALKER, Benjamin. *Hindu World.* London: George Allen & Unwin, 1968

YASHOVIJAYJI, Munishri. *Tirthankar Bhagawan Mahāvira.* 2nd edition. Bombay: Jain Sanskruti Kala Kendra, 1976

III
BUDDHISM

Gautama the Buddha was not only one of the profoundest religious philosophers of this world but also one of its greatest human beings. His life and teachings have been a source of inspiration to millions in many countries for over two thousand five hundred years. He is one of those rare spiritual giants whose name will ever adorn the pages of history. Around that name has grown a vast literature with the result that any writer, who wishes to evaluate afresh the Buddha's achievements, is confronted at the very outset with the almost insoluble problem of sifting the historical and factual elements of his life and teachings from the purely mythical and legendary.

It is believed that Gautama had been preceded by twenty seven other Buddhas and the forthcoming Buddha will be known as the Maitreya Buddha. Therefore Gautama should not be regarded as the founder of a new religion: he is not the *founder* but the *finder* of that timeless Truth that awaits discovery by all who are not enlightened.

In Buddhist literature the Buddha is often referred to as the 'Blessed One' but this term of respect is a serious misnomer. Let us ask the obvious question: "Blessed" by whom? For Buddhahood is not a Divine dispensation; it can be experienced by anyone when the veil of conditioned consciousness is cast aside and the mind is supremely awakened. The word 'Buddha' simply means 'the Awakened or Enlightened One' and much confusion can be avoided if readers abide by this particular meaning.

The gist of the Buddha's message is contained in his famous lines:

"Not to do evil,
To increase good,
To purify the mind;
This is the teaching of the Buddhas."

The last line of this verse implies that the teachings of all the Buddhas were identical or at least more or less the same. One is led to the inevitable conclusion that each Buddha emphasized the importance of virtue and the unconditioning of the mind. It is the function of each Buddha to re-discover these eternal Truths and restate them in the phraseology of his time.

The life of Gautama the Buddha (circa 563-483 B.C.)

Known as 'the Buddha' only after his Enlightenment at the youthful age of twenty nine, Gautama is also respectfully called Sākyamuni ('sage of the Sākyas'), Siddhārtha ('he who has accomplished') and Tathāgata ('he who has arrived at the Truth' or 'thus come' or 'thus gone').

Even before his birth it had been prophesied that Gautama would become either an universal monarch or a person who gives up his royal inheritance to become a Buddha.

Suddhodana, his father, was the chieftain or prince of a Sākyan clan, who ruled over a minor kingdom situated some miles north of Benares. Mahāmāya, his mother, is said to have conceived him after dreaming of the future Buddha descending from heaven in the form of a white elephant and entering her womb.

Gautama was born in the Lumbini Grove, near the ancient town of Kapilavastu in northern India. His birthplace, which is a great centre of Buddhist pilgrimage, was commemorated by the Buddhist Emperor

Asoka who erected there an inscribed pillar.

His mother's untimely death was probably a great blow to the family for she died within a week after her son's birth. Thereafter the child was reared by Mahāprajapati, one of the other wives of his father, who was also the sister of the deceased Mahāmāya. But a foster mother's care can seldom replace that special bond of intimacy and affection that naturally exists between a mother and her own offspring. So one wonders whether the young prince had not been a deprived child in the sense that he hardly enjoyed the comfort, warmth and security of maternal affection. Then again one wonders whether this lack had not been one of the factors that contributed to his feeling of insecurity, which in turn culminated in his forsaking the passing pleasures of the world in the quest for that which is eternal.

It is reported that as a youngster Gautama mastered the various skills and arts that befit a prince, such as proficiency in archery and other sports. Little is known about his boyhood except that he grew up in the lap of royal luxury. The Buddha is said to have referred to those days thus: "I was delicate, O monks, extremely delicate, excessively delicate."

We do not know whether this delicacy was an innate trait or the result of the sumptuous living conditions that were provided him. For his father went to great lengths to surround Gautama's life with all kinds of luxuries and pleasures because he was haunted by the fear that his beloved son might renounce the world as had been prophesied. The prince was given three fine palaces where he could stay during the three different seasons — the summer, the rainy season and the winter.

After marrying Yasodhara he lived with her for a period of about ten years before the birth of their son

Rahula. When the child was born Gautama is supposed to have exclaimed complainingly: "Rahula is born to me!" The word 'Rahula' means 'shackles' and if this incident were true, it would be right to assume that he regarded the advent of a child as a hindrance and obstacle in his own spiritual development. Evidently Rahula was an unwanted child. According to some commentators it was the birth of Rahula that spurred the prince to become an ascetic. But there is a more traditional and popular theory that attributes his renunciation to his seeing a decrepit old man, a diseased man, then a corpse; and finally, a wandering religious monk with a serene countenance. He overreacted to these sights. They awakened him to the truth about the perishability of the body and indeed the impermanence of all mundane things. He started brooding and his heart was filled with the desire to emulate the wandering monk who radiated such peace and happiness.

One night he left home, accompanied by his personal attendant. They crossed a stream together. His loyal attendant sought permission to stay with him but this was refused. Giving up a life of princely comforts, riches and security, Gautama chose the life of solitude, poverty and insecurity in that adventurous quest into the great unknown. This event has rightly been called the Great Renunciation for it entailed an inward journey into the hidden depths of his psyche.

Gautama became an ascetic and for six long and tortuous years in the forests of Uruvela he was engrossed in the 'Great Struggle' of spiritual enquiry. He studied under two famous sages, Alara Kalama and Uddaka Ramaputra, both of whom were highly regarded. Although he learnt everything that they had to offer, he was nevertheless disappointed in their teaching. From Alara he learnt about the state of nothingness, which he succeeded in attaining himself and then became dissatisfied with it. From Uddaka he learnt about the state that is neither-consciousness-nor-unconsciousness but again he was unsatisfied after accomplishing it. Such was Gautama's fastidiousness in spiritual matters that nothing short of perfection, could be acceptable to him.

These six years, however, should not be seen as a period of wasted time and effort because during this period he was involved in self-experimentation and self-enquiry. What he discovered then was to become an integral part of his later teachings.

Gautama fasted frequently and subjected his body to various Yogic austerities because he believed then that asceticism was the surest way to Liberation. He did various breathing exercises which involved the restraining of breathing. In his own words, he did 'practise trance without breathing'. He also severely restricted the intake of food to 'as much as my hollowed palm would hold.' So emaciated did he become that his ribs stuck out, his eyes were deeply sunk in their sockets and when he touched the skin of his stomach he actually held his spine.

During this period he became closely associated with five ascetics and all of them practised austerities together. His poor body became so emaciated that he collapsed one day and was taken to be dead. He then realized that self-mortification was hardly the way to Enlightenment, he abandoned austerities and resumed living as a beggar. Later in life Gautama referred to these years of extreme asceticism as "time spent in endeavouring to tie the air into knots." He realized the importance of avoiding both the extremes of self-indulgence and self-punishment. It is rather by treading the Middle Path of properly caring for the body's health and sensitivity that the mind is kept most alert.

Convinced that self-torture was certainly not the means to self-realization, he started taking food. He ate some milk-rice and beans. When his five companions saw him eating they were so offended that they accused him of giving up striving. They then deserted him and went to the Deer Park in Benares.

After his repudiation by the five ascetics, Gautama became increasingly determined to discover the Truth in his own way. Seated under a Bo-tree (*ficus religiosa*) he resolved: "Never from this seat will I stir, until I have attained the supreme and absolute wisdom."

It is said that during the seven weeks spent under that tree he neither moved from his place nor took any food apart from an offering of milk-rice, provided by a woman called Sujāta.

In the *Anguttara Nikaya* there is a description of the grim determination that animated the Buddha-to be:

> "Two things, bhikkus, I have achieved: not to be self-complacent in good states and not to shrink back weakly in the struggle. Without shrinking back, I struggled on and on. I said to myself: I may be reduced to mere skin, sinews and bones, my flesh and blood may dry up, but I shall win what has not been won. Thus through untiring diligence and endeavour I won awakening; I won total freedom from bondage."

While immersed in a state of deep meditation he attained Enlightenment 'in the last watch of the night.' There is a legend that in the first night-watch he gained a knowledge of all his previous lives; in the second, of all the present states of being; in the third, of the chain of causes and effects; and he became omniscient at the dawn of day. Devout scribes have naturally tended to exaggerate and dramatize what he accomplished.

Not having attained *nirvana* oneself, how can one possibly know with certainty what exactly the Buddha found or experienced? What he discovered will always remain a mystery to those who are still unenlightened and hence for them it becomes a subject of endless speculation and debate.

The triumphant Buddha did not forget his old companions, the five ascetics, who had previously given him up in despair. He went specially to the Deer Park at Benares to meet them. It was to them that he delivered his first sermon of a preaching career that was to last some forty five years. The Master discoursed with all manner of people — high and low, kings and criminals, and seldom indeed was a person not swayed by his noble and powerful personality. Supported by the offerings of the pious, he led the life of a wandering mendicant who discoursed on the eternal truths that he had realized.

Towards the end of his life the Buddha suffered from a serious illness. After he had convalesced, Ananda, his closest devotee, suggested that he should leave behind instructions for the Order of Monks: The Buddha questioned the need for such instructions and added:

> "Be lamps unto yourselves and seek no external refuge. Hold fast to the Truth as a lamp and a refuge."

After the Buddha had partaken of a meal offered by Chunda, a metal worker, he suffered from a fatal attack of dysentery and developed sharp pains. He asked Ananda to accompany him to the jungle town of Kusinara. On their way he rested his weary body between twin trees. Ananda inquired what should be done with the Master's remains. The Buddha said that they should not hinder themselves by honouring his remains, but that they should be zealous, earnest and devote themselves to their own good. Yet there are wise and noble persons who will honour the remains. (Incidentally, why has the Buddhist world over the centuries chosen to disregard the Master's clear remark that the honouring of his remains is an hindrance? Why are his relics worshipped when the Buddha would have preferred otherwise, especially because his teaching that stressed the importance of self-reliantly being a light unto oneself?). Noticing that the Buddha was about to pass away, Ananda could not help weeping for he had been closely associated with him for a long time not only as a devotee, but also as his cousin and personal attendant. The Buddha tried to console him by saying philosophically that separation from all that is near and dear is inevitable. Anything that is born must also pass away.

The dying Buddha told Ananda that some may think that there was no longer a Teacher. But that was not the case; the Truth that he had taught would henceforth be the Teacher. Immediately before his demise the Buddha asked the monks who were by his side to raise any doubts that they had about his teachings lest they reproach themselves afterwards with the thought that they failed to question the Master when they were face to face with him. He made this request thrice but the monks remained silent. They behaved as though they had no doubts whatsoever. Probably they did not wish to trouble the Buddha at his deathbed out of respect, affection and consideration. His last words were:

> "All composite things are subject to decay. Work out your own salvation with diligence."

After his death some of the monks lamented greatly and said that he had died too soon. But those who had a firmer grasp of the teachings reacted to the event calmly with the thought: Everything that is born must of necessity pass away, so how could it be that he too should not pass away?

Boundless Compassion for all

The theme of compassion pervades the entire length and breadth of the Buddha's teachings. The extent to which compassion was highlighted by him has probably never been equalled by any other founder of a religion. He stressed the importance of limitless loving kindness for everyone without any kind of discrimination whatsoever. In the *Metta Sutta* the Buddha eloquently discoursed on compassion:

> "As a mother, even at the risk of her own life, protects her son, her only son, so let him cultivate goodwill without measure among all beings. Let him cultivate goodwill without measure toward the whole world, above, below, around, unstinted, unmixed with any feeling of differing or opposing interests. Let a man remain steadfastly in this state of mind all the while he is awake, whether he be standing, sitting or lying down. This state of heart is the best in the world."

It is easy to remain 'meek and mild' so long as nothing unpleasant happens. But confronted by unpleasantness, hostility and violence, our goodness and composure are tested. Therefore the Buddha continually exhorted his followers to maintain goodwill and love in their hearts, regardless of however badly they are treated by others. Returning enmity for enmity is a conduct absolutely alien to the Buddha's philosophy of courtesy and compassion for all, even under the most trying conditions. Quite in contrast to the maxim that justified revenge by the taking of an eye for an eye and a tooth for a tooth, the compassionate Buddha declared:

> "If a man foolishly wrongs me, I will return to him the protection of my ungrudging love; the more evil emanates from him, the more good shall emanate from me; the fragrance of goodness always comes to me, and the harmful air of evil goes to him."

According to him this philosophy of non-retaliation for evil does not mean that its proponents have to bear suffering in silence for somehow they are not exposed to danger:

> "The virtuous man cannot be hurt, and the misery that the other would inflict returns back to himself."

The Buddha was not a mere preacher because often his life of action was even more eloquent than his lofty precepts. Of the numerous instances that can be cited to illustrate his compassionate behaviour, the following one is noteworthy as it also shows something of his great humility. There was once a surly old monk who suffered from a disease that made the sight and smell of his body so offensive that none wished to go near him, let alone look after him. When the Buddha heard of his plight, he visited the monastery where the monk was staying, asked for some warm water and personally nursed him and continued to do so daily.

The State of Inner Purity

Genuine morality springs from a state of inner purity. Of what value are the seeming charitable acts of a philanthropist, if he were driven by questionable motives such as the craving for power, recognition or fame? For such deeds originate neither in real compassion nor sincere concern for the happiness and welfare of the recipients of his charity. It is a cardinal principle of Buddhist morality that only those acts are pure and *karmaless* which are not tainted by any ulterior motive whatsoever. It is the ethical quality of our minds that solely determines our destinies. We invariably reap the consequences of impure thoughts in the form of sorrow. It is the nature of our thoughts (i.e. Karma) that shapes the present and the future. This doctrine is wonderfully expounded in the opening stanzas of the *Dhammapada*:

> "What we are today flows from our thoughts of yesterday. Our present thoughts determine our life of tomorrow. Our life is the creation of our mind. If a man speaks or acts with an impure mind then suffering follows him."
>
> "If a man speaks or acts with a pure mind then joy follows him."
>
> "He insulted me, he hurt me, he defeated me, he robbed me."
>
> "Those who harbour such thoughts will not be free from hate."
>
> "Those who do not harbour such thoughts will be free from hate."
>
> "For hate is not overcome by hate: hate is overcome by love. This is an eternal law."

The truly virtuous person, in the Buddhist sense of the word, does not bear any grudges and hence is always forgiving. He never allows himself to be contaminated by the evil forces of malice or ill will, because his mind is constantly maintained in a state of unsullied purity.

In the course of explaining his doctrine of righteous living, the Buddha questioned and denounced certain long-revered Hindu practices such as sacrificing animals and bathing in the holy rivers. When a Brahmin, Sundarika Bharadwaja asked the Enlightened One whether he bathed in a certain holy river, he answered that holy rivers cannot wash away evil deeds nor can they make a person holy. But for the pure in heart every day is holy because their deeds are good and they contribute to the security and happiness of all.

On another occasion he spoke to a prince about the utter futility of sacrifices where animals were slain. What is the point of sacrificing poor oxen, goats and fowls? At that time in India animals were sacrificed ritually as a form of atonement for misdeeds or to appease various gods or to safeguard oneself from evil spirits. A genuine sacrifice, in the Buddha's eyes, consists in having right views, right intentions, right speech, right action, right livelihood, right endeavour, right mindfulness and right rapture.

The Five Virtuous Precepts

By observing the Five Precepts (*Pancha Sila*) the Buddhist tries to ensure that his life has a certain sound ethical foundation. These precepts are:

(1) I accept the precept not to kill.
(2) I accept the precept not to steal.
(3) I accept the precept not to commit adultery.
(4) I accept the precept not to lie.
(5) I accept the precept not to take intoxicating liquors or drugs.

These precepts are not commandments in the Judaic-Christian sense; their breach does not entail the commission of any sin. For in Buddhism there is no external authority either in heaven or earth to whom one is answerable for the transgression of anything forbidden. The Buddhist is responsible solely to himself for his actions; he realizes, on the other hand, that he cannot afford to behave irresponsibly because he himself will have to bear the outcome of his thoughts, words and deeds on account of the operation of the law of Karma. These precepts are merely self-imposed resolutions which, if strictly observed, will at least enable his social relationships to be governed by some measure of goodwill and harmony instead of ill will and conflict. Their observance may not necessarily provide him with a passport to *nirvana*, but at least he will become a person of righteous social behaviour and hence a good citizen.

The serious-minded and sincere Buddhist does not make an outward show of the fact that he is conducting his life in the light of the Buddha's teachings. Quite unlike the Sikh, there are no external signs such as wearing a particular dress or hairstyle that help to distinguish him from the rest of society. He is usually content to live anonymously and is not particularly interested in winning converts either. All he aspires after is wisdom and moral rectitude as a means to *nirvana* He behaves self-effacingly, realizing that the self is the greatest illusion that has reduced him to a state of suffering in the seeming endless cycle of births and deaths (*samsāra*).

Does Buddhism Condone or Condemn Meat Eating?

Eating meat was widely prevalent in India in the days of the Buddha. Yet there were certain religious sects such as the Niganthas whose commitment to the doctrine of harmlessness and *ahimsa* (non-injury) was such that they abstained from meat altogether.

Jivaka, a vegetarian monk, asked the Buddha whether the consumption of meat was in accordance with his teachings. The Buddha is reported to have said that provided animals were not seen, heard or suspected to have been *specially* killed for a monk, their meat may be eaten. The killing of living creatures for a Teacher or his disciples results in the formation of demerit or bad Karma. Presumably, then, the only permissible kinds of meat should be from animals that have either not been specially slaughtered for monks or whose deaths were caused by accident, illness or old age.

In his conversation with Siha, the lay Nigantha, the Buddha reiterated the principle that a person is faultless if he eats meat, not knowing that it has been killed or specially prepared for him. He is reported to have said on that occasion that the heart is purified not by the abstinence from flesh but only by the abstinence from lust. Compassion arises not by refusing meat but by radiating the entire world with thoughts of love. When there is such a love the lust to eat meat will die away.

Do Buddhist monks nowadays take the trouble to enquire whether an animal was killed on purpose for them before eating its meat? They surely cannot be unaware of the fact that nearly all the available meat for consumption in modern cities comes from abattoirs. Since the monks are part and parcel of that *particular group* of consumers, does it not follow that the meat they devour with such relish was *specially* made available for them also?

If the only reason that makes me refrain from directly or indirectly killing animals for food is the fear that such actions result in the accumulation of demerit, then does it not indicate that I am not inspired by a compassionate concern for the suffering experienced by animals that are slaughtered but rather by my egoism which is craving for 'spiritual' progress?

Since Buddhists are painfully conscious that the first precept of their religion is 'I accept the precept not to kill', they try to absolve themselves from all moral blame by imagining that they are not vicariously responsible for the destruction of life. For Buddhists, who eat fish, flesh and fowl, justify their dietary practices by resorting to the specious argument that it is the poor fisherman, butcher or hunter who is *solely* responsible for all the killing! Hence it is maintained that demerit is acquired only by those engaged in the actual act of killing! These Buddhists are surely callously indifferent to the fact that they are encouraging these groups of people to amass bad Karma in the course of their occupations and thereby prolonging their misery in *samsāra* or the cycle of births and deaths.

Although the letter of the teachings permit meat eating under certain circumstances, their spirit is somehow more in harmony with vegetarianism than non-vegetarianism. Given the great importance that the Buddha attached to loving kindness to all living beings, it is a great pity that he failed to enjoin the members of his Order and lay disciples to avoid meat under *all* circumstances. We have seen that he allowed the eating of meat only when an animal has not been specially killed. For the helpless animals that are subjected to the agony of slaughter, does it make much difference whether they are being specially killed or otherwise?

For centuries Buddhist scholars have furiously debated whether the grave illness that preceded the Buddha's death was precipitated by the eating of pork, as the non-vegetarians maintain, or, the eating of truffles, as the vegetarians insist. The truth will always remain obscure or unknown. Indeed the available records of the Buddha's life and sayings are shrouded in a mist of legends and interpolations. But sometimes bright rays of light manage to penetrate the mist and give us an inkling of what the original wisdom might have been, such as the following lines from *The Dhammapada:*

> "All beings tremble before danger, all fear death. When a man takes this into account, he does not kill or cause to kill."
>
> "All beings fear before danger, life is dear to all. When a man takes this into account, he does not kill or cause to kill."

So is it not incumbent upon every conscientious Buddhist to eat only such food in the production of which 'he does not kill or *cause to kill*'?

Cast aside Caste

The society that the Buddha taught was deeply divided and plagued by the caste system, much like that of modern India. The arrogance and hauteur of those born into the privileged 'superior' castes was in sharp contrast to the social disadvantages that were thrust upon those born into the humiliated 'inferior' castes.

Although the Buddha himself hailed from the uppermost warrior-ruler Kshatriya caste (the Kshatriyas in his day enjoyed a higher status than the Brahmin priestly caste, for Brahmins were then considered 'low-born'), he nevertheless used forceful language to condemn an iniquitous system that reduced large sections of the population to a status of perpetual subjection:

> 'No man is noble by birth,
> No man is ignoble by birth.
> Man is noble by his own deeds,
> Man is ignoble by his own deeds."

Thus a kind hearted 'untouchable' is far nobler than

an unscrupulous Brahmin who claims Divine descent. Had so revolutionary a teaching been accepted, it would surely have shattered the age-old structure of Indian society. So it is not at all surprising that India conveniently turned its back on Buddhism.

All countries with hereditary and powerful aristocracies should be looked at sceptically because it is only by their conduct towards the less privileged classes that their nobility should be determined. It is hardly the Buddha's fault that his 'followers' in Buddhist countries do not heed his words. Even in Sri Lanka (Ceylon), the soi-disant 'leading Buddhist country in the world' where the teachings are supposedly preserved in their 'pristine purity', it is appalling that social relations are characterised by anything but harmony and goodwill. Those belonging to 'low' castes are downtrodden and the internecine tribal conflict between the Sinhalese and Tamils has resulted in much bloodshed.

Since the Buddha refused to recognize caste distinctions, he admitted into the Order of monks persons not only from the 'high' castes but also from the 'low', such as Sunita, the 'outcaste'. The spirit of true egalitarianism knows no frontiers: it is all-embracing in he sense that it totally disregards not only caste disinctions, but also all other divisions based on race, colour, economic status, class, nationality, sex and the like.

Ananda, often described as the Buddha's 'favourite disciple' (one wonders whether he had any such favourites because presumably he loved all alike), once requested water from Pakati, a girl of 'low' caste. The embarrassed girl said: "O, nobleman, as I belong to the Matanga caste, I am too humble and mean to serve you water." Ananda quipped: "Sister, what I requested was not caste but water!"

Opposition to Miracles

When a so-called religious leader's message lacks the intrinsic power of persuasion and conviction, then he usually resorts to extrinsic device of impressing gullible folk by performing miracles. It is to the credit of the Buddha that he condemned miracles in no uncertain terms.

The Buddha turned down Kevaddha's request that he should instruct a member of his Order to perform a miracle at Nalanda so that he might get more followers. Thereupon he discoursed on the three kinds of miracles: The Miracle of Mysteries, that gives one the ability to become invisible and pass through solid walls as well as walk on water; the Miracle of Secrets, that enables one to find out the contents of others' hearts and minds. He strongly disapproved of such miracles. But, above all, there is the Miracle of Education whereby one gets awakened after hearing the preaching of a Buddha.

The scriptures record an interesting conversation between the Buddha and his disappointed disciple Sunakkhatta who had decided to leave him. He was no longer going to regard the Buddha as the Master since he worked no miracles. The Buddha characteristically answered this criticism by saying that the purpose of his preaching the Truth was the destruction of evil: the performance of miracles was hardly his objective. Then Sunakkhatta also accused the Buddha of not revealing the origin of the world. Then the Master said that neither was that the aim of the Truth he taught and he reiterated the point that the goal of his teaching was the elimination of evil.

Once a disciple enquired whether there were no miraculous and wonderful things. The Buddha replied that the monk who renounced the transient pleasures of the world for the eternal bliss of holiness performed the only miracle that was worthy of being so described. Whereas the desire to perform miracles arose either from covetousness or vanity, the person who renounces thereby unburdens himself of Karma.

The Buddhist scriptures have several references to miraculous deeds that were supposedly performed by the Buddha. Was the Buddha discouraging the performance of miracles by others and at the same time hypocritically performing them himself? Numerous awe-inspiring stories of miracles have helped to invest his personality with an air of mysterious superhumanity, as though he were some kind of deity or celestial being from the world of religious fiction, whereas he was actually just another human being but admittedly one who had accomplished something extraordinary. In the light of his clearly expressed views on miracles, must one not question the authenticity of such scriptural accounts?

Why ask Fruitless Questions

It had become common among certain philosophers to indulge in vain speculations about the nature of the Absolute and other matters. But the Buddha discouraged such speculation, especially because it served no useful purpose. The Buddha categorically refused to express an opinion when Potthapada confronted him with the Ten Indeterminates:

(1) Is the world eternal?
(2) Is the world not eternal?
(3) Is the world infinite?
(4) Is the world not infinite?
(5) Is the soul the same as the body?
(6) Is the soul different from the body?
(7) Is there an afterlife?
(8) Is there no afterlife?

(9) Does one both live again and not live again?
(10) Does one neither live again nor not live again?

Such questions, said the Buddha, are neither concerned with the Truth nor do they contribute to right conduct, detachment, purification and tranquillity. They do not lead to Enlightenment.

Did the sage react evasively to Potthapada's questions because he did not know the answers himself? Probably, as he said, he regarded it an utter waste of precious time and energy to become involved in problems that are beyond the comprehension of the limited human intellect. These problems, if ever solved, may perhaps make the solver a more knowledgeable person but not necessarily wiser nor morally superior. It was not that the Buddha was opposed to contemplation, for he himself had forsaken the comforts of a princely life to lead a contemplative one. What moved him at that time to take that step was certainly not a sterile intellectual curiosity that lacked seriousness and personal involvement. On the contrary, he had been consumed with a burning passion to unravel the mystery of suffering, its nature and origin as well as its total elimination. When the house is on fire why bother to speculate about how the fire began, when one's only concern should be its immediate extinguishment? On account of this attitude he naturally frowned upon all philosophical questions that had no relevance to ultimate Emancipation.

Evidently the Buddha knew much more than what he chose to teach: what he expounded was only a small fragment of his vast understanding. It would have been very interesting for posterity had he expressed his views on a greater variety of topics but he wisely confined his teachings only to the fundamental issue of spiritual freedom. On one occasion when he was staying in the Simsapa Grove he held a few simsapa leaves in his hand and asked: 'Brothers, which are more numerous, the leaves that I hold or those in the grove?' He was answered with the comment that the leaves he was holding were very few in number in contrast to those in the grove. Thereupon he discoursed: "Just so, brothers, the things I have revealed to you are few, very few, in comparison with those things which I have known and understand but not revealed to you ... I have revealed that there is sorrow everywhere, that desire is the cause of sorrow . . . I have revealed only what is conducive to the perfect state, only what is concerned with the holy life, only what results in the cessation of bondage and leads to perfect calm, to perfect wisdom — *nirvana*."

You are Your Own Saviour

In the teachings of the Buddha there are no doctrinal dogmas that have to be blindly accepted, and which if unaccepted might result in eternal damnation or excommunication. There is also no provision for a central ecclesiastical authority with the right to determine whether a particular interpretation of the teaching is a heresy or otherwise.

There is no principle of Buddhism that is based on 'Divine revelation' or 'Divine decree'. Only when the accuracy of a truth is verifiable by human intelligence does it become acceptable. Truth is its own proof. This scientific approach to spiritual investigation is one of the outstanding features of Buddhism; it is a characteristic that is all the more invaluable because rarely, almost never, is it found in other religious systems.

The Buddha always refused to discuss the question of the existence of God or Creator. Theistic systems insist that man should demonstrate his utter subservience to God through sacrifice, prayer and *puja*. In Buddhism, however, there is no God who has to be appeased or bribed in order to win favours. What is the point of praying when no Divine Being exists to listen to our prayers? The onus is wholly on man to cleanse himself through and through of all traces of Karma, and to realize *nirvana*. Buddhist doctrine never urges man to reduce himself to a docile creature in fearful recognition of God's omnipotence but rather it emphasises the importance of hard work as a prelude to self-realization. Those who rely on external aids become weaklings whereas through self-reliance one grows from strength to strength.

When the Buddha appealed to each individual 'to work out your salvation with diligence', he was obviously implying that salvation was well within the ken of human possibility; in other words, salvation can be found unaided, as he himself had done. Salvation is not a blessing conferred by God; it is the outcome of self-examination and meditation. But few are interested in exerting themselves in this manner. The vast majority would much rather find comfort and consolation in beliefs and dogmas that promise an easy 'salvation' vicariously, such as the belief that Jesus redeemed the sins of all mankind through his crucifixion.

To regard the Buddha as 'the Saviour of the World' is to do him a great injustice, for nothing is more alien to his teaching than the expectation to be liberated through the instrumentality of another. Are we not our own saviours?

The Buddha eschewed all forms of dependence and stressed the importance of self-reliance. If his words in the *Mahā Parinibbāna Sutta* were taken seriously, it is incumbent upon man to free himself of the desire to be helped by gurus, priests and intercessors:

> "Be lamps unto yourselves. Be a refuge to yourselves. Resort to no external refuge. Hold fast to the Truth as a lamp. Hold fast to the Truth as a refuge. Look not for refuge to anyone besides yourselves."

One should have thought that even looking up to the Buddha would be contrary to the spirit of his teaching insofar as one would thereby be seeking the refuge of someone other than oneself. Yet in the Buddhist world this teaching of absolute independence is openly flouted. Given below are only a few instances of such violations:

First, the 'Pansil' ceremony of promising to observe the five precepts is preceded by a thrice repeated declaration:

> I take refuge in the Buddha
> I take refuge in the Dhamma (teachings)
> I take refuge in the Sangha (brotherhood of monks).

Second, statues and pictures of the Buddha in temples, homes and public places are worshipped. Offerings of incense, flowers and the like are made as though the Buddha were another Hindu god. Equally deplorable is worshipping the Buddha's relics, which practice is strangely considered as being particularly meritorious.

The Great Illusion of the Self

The Buddhist doctrine of *anatta* or no-soul is unique because it is not found in any other religion. The Buddha emphasized this teaching unequivocally:

> "Whether Buddhas arise in this world or not, it always remains a fact that the constituent parts of a being are lacking in a soul."

The Buddha's insistence on the non-existence of an individual permanent soul or *ātman* was a radical departure from traditional Hindu thought that had maintained its existence. What is the self or the soul? According to the *Brhadāranyaka Upanishad* this *ātman* is unseizable, indestructible and unattached; it is also not bound, does not tremble and is not injured. Hindus believe that although the body chemically disintegrates at death yet the soul remains deathless and then migrates to another body, unless it has already got merged in *Brahman*, the Supreme Reality or the Absolute. The concepts of *ātman* and *Brahman* are closely associated; they are in fact two aspects of the same reality for *ātman* is only the subjective aspect of what is objectively called *Brahman*.

Why does man delude himself with this belief in an immortal soul or self? Is it not because of the failure to realise that his self or psychological personality is only a temporary composition of different parts, a mere bundle of attributes, that may disintegrate at any moment? How can a transitory aggregation of qualities ever have the quality of permanency? What is erroneously regarded as the 'self' is made up of five attributes called *skandhas*. These are form (*rupa*), sensation (*vedanā*), perception (*sannā*), volition (*sankhāra*) and consciousness (*vinnāna*). How can there be anything permanent because these *skandhas* are constantly moving and changing like the waters of a swiftly flowing river?

The impermanency of all things is a cardinal tenet of Buddhism. Those who miss this are unnecessarily going to make themselves unwise and unhappy. An extract from a well-known verse that is chanted at Buddhist funerals is noteworthy:

> "Impermanent are all conditioned things;
> Their nature is to rise and pass away;
> They come to pass, they cease."

What is called the mind is the result of an amalgamation of various bodily and psychological and social influences. There are the inherited racial and biological dispositions and the acquired attitudes, prejudices and beliefs. One is also conditioned by the innumerable experiences of an entire lifetime. All these influences have made a man what he is, they have given him a sense of personality. I am therefore conscious of my 'self'. Hence I feel separate from my neighbour and he also feels alienated from me because we both foolishly entertain the illusion of the self. When he tries to promote his self-interest and I try to promote mine, an otherwise friendly relationship soon gets spoilt by feelings of suspicion and hostility. This belief in a separate self makes us selfish, which is the primary cause of sorrow. But if the mind were thoroughly stripped of all these numerous influences, will not the 'self' which is the collective outgrowth of these influences, also cease to be? In exploding the myth of the 'self' the Buddha was also pointing his finger to the cause of all social conflict.

Reflections on Karma and Rebirth

The doctrine of transmigration and the associated doctrine of Karma were already there before the advent of Buddhism. Buddhism conveniently adopted these doctrines, adapted them and made them harmonize with its own special character.

Karma is a natural law that operates in the universe; it is a law in itself in the sense that it is entirely independent of any external power, human or divine. It is a law with no known beginning nor was it promulgated by any authority. It is not that one should 'obey' the law of Karma but rather recognize its existence and live intelligently in the light of that understanding.

According to the theory of Karma a man's misfortunes

are directly traceable to his immoral actions in this life or a previous one, but not all circumstances and psychological attitudes originate solely in Karma. Probably it was the existence of this moral element that made the theory so acceptable to Buddhist thought. The reason why a person gets brutally assassinated is probably because he had been guilty of murder in a former life. When A shoots B then B is only suffering the consequence of a moral crime that he had previously committed. If we believe in this kind of reasoning then society is not obliged to punish A because the law of Karma will ensure that A pays for what he has done, By the same token, why engage in social welfare work and improve the living conditions of the poor and downtrodden, because the socially underprivileged deserve all that suffering which was caused by their owr bad Karma? If these unfortunate folk were helped, would they not be deprived of the opportunity of undergoing hardships and thereby cancelling out the consequences of their bad Karma caused by their own past misbehaviour? We can see why the theory of Karma is so popular in Buddhist countries because it can be conveniently used to justify apathy and inaction in the face of abject poverty and social injustice.

This kind of callous indifference to the miserable plight of others arises from a gross misunderstanding of Buddhism in general and the doctrine of Karma in particular. The actions of a genuine Buddhist are never devoid of consideration, kindness and generosity. With compassionate altruism he will try hard to alleviate all distress either by acting individually or as a member of a group.

Many writers fallaciously equate the doctrine of Karma with predestination. While it is true that Karma means the law of cause and effect, it does not follow that the relationship between the cause and its effect is unalterably fixed. Admittedly the present has been shaped by the past and the future will be shaped by the present but it does not follow that neither present nor future cannot be changed. The force of Karma can be modified; indeed the chain of Karma can be broken. Let us illustrate this point by considering the example of a seed such as an acorn that can only germinate in the form of an oak tree. The relationship between the acorn (cause) and the oak tree (effect) is predetermined. The acorn is botanically conditioned to produce an oak tree and nothing else. That kind of fatalism does not operate in the sphere of Karma. For any person can turn over a new leaf by discarding once and for all the entire burden of Karma and find Enlightenment.

In the Buddhist literature probably the best example of a person experiencing the spiritual metamorphosis of Enlightenment is that of the notorious robber Angulimala. His peculiar predilection was killing people with the intention of collecting their fingers. He terrorised villages and was feared throughout the land. When the Buddha heard of Angulimala's bloodthirsty activities, he wanted to meet him personally but his followers implored him never to visit this dangerous man. Despite their warnings the Buddha approached him fearlessly and explained to him the utter folly of his crimes. Angulimala listened to the Master's words and understood the Truth. As a result of that realization he was relieved of the entire burden of his past Karma of wicked deeds and thereupon found Enlightenment.

What is it that is reborn? According to popular Hindu theology there is a subtle entity, vaguely called the 'soul', which leaves the body at death and takes residence in a new body, like a traveller moving from one hotel to another.

The Buddhist concept, however, is that there is no

such thing as a deathless soul that transmigrates from one body to another. It is rather the *craving* or *psychological traits* that were still active at the time of the death of one body that causes the same set of psychological traits to emerge in a new body. So the mind of a newly born baby is not an innocent *tabula rasa* but one that is already heavily conditioned by these inherited tendencies (i.e. Karma).

All these traits collectively constitute our 'personality' or 'ego'. Some of the most potent of these traits are our ambitions, frustrations, fears, hopes, desires, likes, aversions and the like. Now, the idea that it is these traits that manifest themselves in a new body is based on several assumptions: First, we know that our traits are recorded and preserved in the brain cells and remain there so long as the brain is alive, unless their erasure was caused by a reason such as a brain injury. At death do these traits disappear along with the brain? It is assumed that these traits can exist independently of their extinct brain. Second, it is also assumed that these traits are transferable. Material possessions are certainly passable from person to person but is this also true of psychological traits that are supposedly communicable from the dead to the living?

The theory of rebirth, in other words, is founded on the suppositions that psychological traits, probably because they are a form of matter, can divest themselves from the brain cells at death and then travel on their own to another brain and eventually become a part of the consciousness of a newly born person or any other living being.

A popular practice among many Buddhists is the performance of good works, such as giving alms to the needy, in order to accumulate good or meritorious Karma. They believe that their store of good Karma will somehow stand them in good stead sometime in the future; it is also believed, incidentally, that the merit so accrued can be transferred to deceased friends and relatives so that they may also benefit from it, just in case they have been reborn in unfortunate circumstances or lower forms of life. But seldom is it realised that 'merit transfer' is inconsistent with the well-known Buddhist maxim 'you are your own saviour'.

Although good Karma is obviously preferable to bad Karma, it should be emphasised that the state of *nirvana* is free of all forms of Karma. The Buddha explained that all volitional acts result in the creation of Karma:

"I declare that volition (*chetana*) is Karma."

To avoid confusion it is necessary to indicate here that in Sanskrit the word *chetana* means consciousness whereas in Buddhist literature it stands for volition.

Any action propelled by an intention, determined by a psychological trait, results inevitably in the formation of Karma. Only motiveless action is without Karma. The deeds of a liberated person (*arhat*) or a Buddha are without Karma in the sense that they are performed for their own sake without any ulterior motive whatsoever, such as, say, the expectation of a reward or the desire for recognition. Such deeds are pure and without Karma since they spring from the indescribable state of creative emptiness.

The Peace of Nirvana

No words can adequately convey the nature and significance of *nirvana* but something of its flavour is noticeable in the following extracts from a few important Buddhist sources. Probably the finest description of *nirvana* is contained in the *Udana* which takes the form of a series of negative statements:

"O brothers! there is an abode where there is no earth nor water nor air".

"There is an abode, O brothers! where there is no world of infinity-of-space nor world of infinity-of-intelligence nor world of cognition or non-cognition nor this world nor the world yonder, neither sun nor moon."

"That abode, O brothers! has neither coming nor going, neither birth nor death. Without origin and without annihilation and beyond thought is that. The destruction of all sorrow is that."

"That abode, O brothers! is unborn, uncreated, unmanifested and unconditioned. Unless it were that, there could not be cognised in this world birth, creation, manifestation and conditioning."

"That abode is *Nirvana*."

According to the *Lankavatara Sutta*:

"*Nirvana* is not to be found by mental searching . . ."

The *Suttanipata* states:

"That monk of wisdom here, devoid of desire and passion, attains to deathlessness, peace, the uncharging state of *nirvana* ... The steadfast go out like this lamp . . . Where there is no-thing, where nothing is grasped, this is the Isle of No-beyond. *Nirvana* do I call it — the utter extinction of aging and dying."

The *Samyutta-Nikaya* also attempts to describe it.

"The stopping of becoming is *nirvana* . . . It is

> called *nirvana* because of the getting rid of craving."

In the *Ariya Pariyesana Sutta* the Buddha contrasted the transitoriness of mundane pursuits with *nirvana* which alone is eternal and hence worthy of achievement. There are, he said, two quests: the noble and the ignoble. Man, being himself subject to decay, disease, sorrow and death, is given to the pursuit of ignoble things such as wanting a wife, children, property and the like. All these things are fleeting and impermanent. But the quest for *nirvana* is noble because it alone is not subject to decay, disease, sorrow and death.

There is an unmistakeable suggestion that *nirvana* is a state of deathless bliss in an insecure world of continual change.

Etymologically, the word '*nirvana*' means 'blown out': *nir* stands for the negative and *va* for 'to blow'. *Nirvana* is popularly likened to a lamp that has got blown out. There is surely no 'blower' or 'I' that does the blowing, but it would seem that the lamp gets blown out of its own accord when it is devoid of the oil of the illusion of the 'I' that everlastingly seeks continuance. When the 'I' with its attendant *becoming* process ceases, there is the 'I'-less state of *being*. When perception is no longer restricted, perverted and distorted by the tunnel vision emanating from the 'I', what remains is the liberated, unconditioned state of pure seeing —. the dimension of Reality where things are seen as they truly are. Some writers have called it 'annihilation'. But strictly speaking there was never a permanent entity or 'annihilator' that did the work of annihilation. Was it the 'I' that was annihilated?
The 'I' cannot get annihilated because, having been a non-fact or an illusion, it never *actually* existed in the first place. Yet in another sense the 'I' had existed but

only as a figment of the imagination.

Nirvana may be described as that extraordinary state of clarity wherein all illusions or non-facts have totally disappeared and can never arise again.

Nirvana is that supreme state of absolute freedom wherein the mind is no longer driven by the ceaseless and insatiable demands of the ego. When all sense of individuality gets discarded there comes into being a certain universality of outlook. There is an untrammelled intelligence a heightened awareness that one is part and parcel of the entire cosmos. Above all, *nirvana* may also be described as that new spiritual dawning in which one radiates boundless compassion to all because the petty 'I' with its self-centred pursuits has altogether ceased.

Throughout the centuries numerous scholars, philosophers and monks have hotly debated the nature of *nirvana*. Their arguments were invariably based on their concepts about something that cannot be contained within the confines of mere concepts. If *nirvana* were 'beyond thought', then it is probably in some unknown realm that is far outside the reach of the mind. One sees immediately the futility of speculating about it since thinking is an activity of the conditioned thought-process whereas *nirvana* is a pure 'unconditioned' state.

The mind can move from thought to thought, from the known to the known, but can it ever transcend the boundaries of the known and enter the sphere of the unknown? When the Buddhist aspires after *nirvana*, which cannot be sought and captured by the intellect, is he not indulging in wishful thinking? Is he not also getting himself entrapped in the *karmic* process of becoming?

In the Buddhist world a view that is widely held is that the Buddha took some five hundred odd lives to perfect himself. It is believed that the road to *nirvana* is so long and arduous that it can be reached only by a process of gradual evolution. This outlook has unfortunately contributed to a certain lethargy amongst Buddhists. Consequently many of them seem to lack a sense of religious urgency. They hardly become seriously discontented with their long-suffering bondage to the law of Karma. So it is heartening to find a statement in the *Sutta Pitaka* that *nirvana* is attainable right here and now, in this very life itself:

> "The wise man, who clings to nothing and rejoices in his freedom from attachment, who has conquered his appetites, will win *nirvana* even in this world."

Who has the patience to endure sorrow for an indefinite period of time? Let us rejoice that there is the possibility of immediate realization, instantaneous spiritual transformation as it were in the twinkling of an eye. So if we fail to find the release of Enlightenment in this present life we have only ourselves to blame.

SELECT BIBLIOGRAPHY

BYLES, M.B. *Footprints of Gautama the Buddha*. London: Rider, 1957

The Dhammapada. Harmondsworth: Penguin Books, 1977

DIKSHIT, Sudhakar. *Sermons and Sayings of the Buddha*. 2nd edition. Bombay: Chetana, 1977

Encyclopaedia of Religion and Ethics; edited by James Hastings. Edinburgh: T. & T. Clark,

JINARAJADASA, C. *Buddha and His Message*. Adyar: Theosophical Publishing House, 1948

JINARAJADASA, C. *The Reign of Law in Buddhism (Buddhist essays).* 2nd edition. Adyar: Theosophical Publishing House, 1948

KIRTHISINGHE, Buddhadasa P. The Buddha. His Democratic and Basic Human Rights (In *Contemporary Review* Vol. 244 No.1418 March 1984)

MALALASEKERA, G.P. *The Buddha and His Teachings.* (Colombo). Lanka Bauddha Mandalaya, 1957

PARRINDER, Geoffrey. *The Wisdom of the Early Buddhists.* New York: New Directions Publishing Corporation, 1977

POTTER, C.F. *The Great Religious Leaders.* New York: Simon and Schuster, 1958

Religions of India. New Delhi: Clarion Books,

RHYS DAVIDS, T.W. *Early Buddhism.* London: Archibald Constable, 1908

RICE, Edward. *Eastern Definitions.* New York: Doubleday, 1978

Sayings of Buddha. New York: Peter Pauper Press, 1957

SPIEGLBERG, Fredric. *Living Religions of the World.* London: Thames and Hudson, 1957

WALKER, Benjamin. *Hindu World.* London: George Allen & Unwin, 1968 *The World's Great Religions.* New York: Time, 1957

IV
SIKHISM

Sikhism, the youngest religion of India, is indeed the latest flowering of Hindu mysticism, a new culmination of the Bhakti movement that prevailed in the country during the fifteenth century. However, unlike the other streams of the Bhakti movement, Sikhism rejected all ritualism and the concept of *avataras* (incarnations), laying sole emphasis on God as the Impersonal Absolute that does not take birth. Sikhism also rejected the caste system and developed a refreshing outlook of universality then unknown to any other faith in India.

Although the Sikhs constitute just some two per cent of India's population, they wield much power and influence in Indian society, particularly because they are well represented in the civil service as well as the armed forces. Their material prosperity may be attributed to the fact that they are largely concentrated in the East Punjab, one of the most fertile agricultural regions of the country. Their long-cherished memories of having been the victims of religious persecution and torture under the Muslim rule in India provide important psychological factors that have perhaps contributed to the evolution of their notion of a Sikh nation. The practice of Sikhism is no longer confined to India, because the Sikhs took with them their religion, language and culture wherever they have settled down overseas. There are today large numbers of Sikh emigrants in Malaysia, East Africa, the United Kingdom as well as parts of the U.S.A. and Canada. The stately and well-built Sikh, bearded and turbaned, is a common sight in many a Western city.

Foundational Scriptures

The foundational scriptures of Sikhism are the *Adi Granth* and *Japji*.

The *Adi Granth*, commonly known as *Granth Sahib*, complied by Guru Arjan, the fifth Guru, is the authoritative scripture of the Sikhs. It is a voluminous book of more than 1400 large size pages in the Gurmukhi script, comprising of songs (*bani*) not only by the Sikh Gurus but also by Hindu and Muslim saints as well as by numerous bards who composed verses between the twelfth and seventeenth centuries.

Strangely for the times in which it was written or compiled, *Adi Granth* propagates the ideal of one universal faith, a world-religion that cuts across the borders of castes and creeds and gives prime importance to attainment of spiritual greatness by following the path of truthful living, contentment and humility.

This great scripture of Sikhism presents before us a sort of parliament of preceptors and saints belonging to various beliefs who speak to us on behalf of *man*, irrespective of his country or language. Among the Hindu saints whose devotional poems are found in the *Adi Granth* are Jaidev, Namdev, Ravidas, Ramananda, Beni, Pipa, Paramananda and others. Kabir's contribution to this work comprises 292 hymns as against 974 from Guru Nanak, 907 from Guru Amardas and 2218 from Guru Arjan Dev, its compiler. The *Granth* also includes poems by Farid, a noted Sufi saint.

In spite of this multiplicity and diversity of the contributors to the *Adi Granth* there is a perfect homogeneity in the Central theme of the work — fatherhood of God and brotherhood of man. Although not a philosophical treatise as such, the *Adi Granth* preaches a religion dedicated to devotion and complete surrender to the will of God. And the Sikh conception of God is All Love, All Truth, All Wisdom — God who is unchanging and immutable, immortal, unborn and self-existent.

> "God is unfathomable, inconceivable. He is the Highest of High, infinite without end" — *Guru Arjan Dev*.

Japji

While the *Adi Granth* is a compilation of devotional songs and hymns, *Japji* is a prose work of great significance composed by Guru Nanak, the founder of Sikhism. This work is rightly considered as the quintessence of the Sikh religion. *Japji* comprises only 38 paragraphs (*pauris*) with a prologue and an epilogue.

Guru Nanak (1469-1539)

Born in Talwandi, about 30 miles from Lahore, the founder of Sikhism was named Nanak Nirakari. It is interesting that this name itself is not without spiritual significance for it means 'Nanak, servant of the Formless one'.

Nanak was a contemporary of Martin Luther in distant Europe. Both were religious reformers, in the sense that they were highly critical of certain questionable practices being then perpetrated in the name of religion. Nanak, however, was not merely a religious reformer but the inaugurator of an entirely new religion.

His father was a petty merchant, farmer and land-steward who had duties to perform for the owner of the village, Rāe Bulār, a Muslim Rajput. Even at the tender age of five Nanak was talking about God; he was indeed precocious and well-versed in the Hindu scriptures. When he was sent to the village primary school at the age of seven he often embarrassed his teacher by asking such profound questions. as wanting to know the esoteric meaning of the first letter of the alphabet. The child had a dreamy and meditative disposition and was in this respect quite different from other children who were more keen on playing games. So dreamy was he that he lost everything that he took out of the house, which very much annoyed his father. At school he learned the current Hindi dialect as well as Sanskrit; he also studied Persian in order to prepare himself for his father's post of village accountant.

After leaving school he sought the company of holy men and visited religious mendicants in his neighbourhood. His father's efforts to make him do some sort of work proved fruitless.

When Nanak was nine it was arranged to place around his neck a *janeu* or the sacred thread of the twice-born, in accordance with Hindu religious custom. As the priest was about to perform the ceremony before a large gathering of people, the boy seized the thread from the priest's hand and questioned its usefulness. The youngster was already showing signs of independence, individuality and nonconformity in religious matters. The priest explained that without the thread he would be a low-class person, for the *janeu* conferred caste superiority. Thereupon Nanak surprized the assembled people by offering his own special interpretation of the significance of the *janeu*:

> "Make mercy your cotton, contentment your thread, continence its knot, truth its twist.
> That would be a *janeu* for the soul."
>
> "If you have such a thread, O Brahmin, then put if one me. It will not rupture or become soiled or get burnt or lost."

The priest observed that the boy would be 'a person without religion' unless he wore the thread. Nanak retorted that all around them were thieves, adulterers and liars despite their wearing the *Janeu*! He said that no string could ensure purity of action. True religion consisted in man's relationship to God.

Nanak's father was already disappointed in the boy who was now aged seventeen. But he begged his father to trust him. Thereupon the father gave him twenty rupees and strictly enjoined him to spend it on business in a nearby village. Nanak who had set out to do some trade met a company of religious devotees and spent all his money on them! When he returned home empty-handed, the exasperated father slapped him so violently that his cheeks became blue.

The father's persuasions to make him work ended in failure. For instance, when it was suggested that he should help cultivate the farm, Nanak replied:

> "Make your body the field, good works the seed, irrigate with God's name; make your heart the cultivator; God will germinate in your heart, and you shall thus obtain *nirvana*."

This reply was characteristic of Nanak who showed no interest in worldly pursuits. When it became clear that he was not going to settle down to any regular employment, it was planned to send him to Sultānpur where his sister lived.

With the intention of diverting Nanak's interest from spiritual to mundane matters, his parents got him married at the young age of sixteen years. This union bore him two sons. But even marriage and children failed to alter his essential religious temperament. When his mother asked him to give up his endless meditations, it is reported that he lay down for four days and declared that he would die if he were deprived of the name of God.

On the recommendation of his brother-in-law he

found employment in Sultanpur as a storekeeper in the Government service. It is said that he not only worked efficiently and was entirely free from corruption, but also gave away most of his earnings to the needy.

This was the time when Mardana, a minstrel, joined him and became his personal attendant. They were devoted to each other and at night they sang hymns composed by Nanak while Mardana played the rebeck.

An encounter with God

An extraordinary and deeply moving spiritual experience often becomes the great turning point in the life of many a mystic. It is the kind of rare and sublime experience that inspires them with such a heightened sense of mission that it naturally determines the subsequent course of their lives. In the case of Nanak, after his morning bath in the river on August 20, 1507, at the age of thirty-eight, he was 'taken in a vision to God's presence' when God himself is said to have spoken to him thus: "Go and repeat my name and cause others to do so. Live uncontaminated by the world. Practise the repetition of my name, charity, ablutions, worship and meditation."

Three days after receiving this divine message he resigned his post, gave away all his possessions to the poor and thence began his lifework as a wandering preacher-cum-bard, accompanied by his musician friend Mardana.

Forsaking his wife and sons and renouncing the comforts of hearth and home, he travelled extensively to what were then considered distant places — Assam, Ceylon (Sri Lanka), Mecca and Tibet.

The literature of Sikhism is replete with detailed accounts of Nanak's activities during the course of his long travels — visits to holy places, meetings with all sorts of persons and the ensuing conversations, arguments and spiritual discourses. There are also fascinating narratives of miracles ascribed to him. For example, at Delhi he is said to have raised to life a dead elephant. Yet when Emperor Sikandar Lodi asked him to repeat this feat for his amusement he allowed the poor animal to die again, and said: "It is God alone who destroys as well as brings to life."

Who can say whether such events did actually happen in the sense that they are historically accurate, or that they are merely the inventions of pious devotees who eagerly desired the outside world to view their religious leader in a superhuman light? One wonders whether the reported 'wonderful deeds' of his are not purely allegorical.

The story of Nanak's life has been so embellished with various miracles he is supposed to have performed that it is difficult to ascertain the true facts. Is there any corpus of sacred literature where zealous scribes have not tended to invest the founders of religions with supernatural powers? Nothing fosters the fervour of the faithful more than graphic accounts of the extraordinariness of their religious leaders. Gullibility is the outstanding feature of the believer whereas scepticism is that of the critical investigator. In the case of Nanak, probably all the fables in various biographical accounts merely provided the settings for his numerous verses and utterances.

Even in the dress he chose to wear Nanak bore witness to his famous aphorism: "There is no Hindu, there is no Musalman." For often he combined the dress of the Hindu sadhu with that of the Muslim fakir. He probably looked very striking and strange, for he wore a Muslim headdress along with a Hindu yellow robe which was covered by a long white scarf. He had a bone necklace and carried a rosary. It has become customary to depict him as a wise old man with a flowing white beard. People who met Nanak may also have deemed it significant that his two faithful companions belonged to the two rival religions of the day in India for Mardana was a Muslim and Bala a Hindu.

Is meat eating ethical?

It is reported that on one occasion when Nanak was hungry he had cooked and eaten a portion of venison of a deer that had been given him. He thereby openly flouted the orthodox Hindu dietetic rule of vegetarianism. When he was criticised for eating flesh, he said that it was foolish for man who was born of flesh and lived continually in the flesh to object to eating flesh. But those who were most careful about not eating meat sometimes ate men by being oppressive!:

> "Those who have given up meat and cannot stand even its flavour, eat men in the darkness of the night."

He was obviously trying to stress the importance of compassion in human relationships for there is no virtue in the life of a sanctimonious vegetarian who is heartless and behaves selfishly by exploiting people. Vegetarianism by itself is meaningless, unless it is the expression of a life of goodness and love. Nevertheless are not vegetarians at least refusing to be contributory parties to the suffering and agony experienced by helpless animals that end up in slaughterhouses? Genuine compassion knows no frontiers and surely it includes concern for the welfare and lives of not only human beings but all the living creatures.

After disguising himself as a Muslim pilgrim, Nanak went to Mecca. There an Arab priest found him sleeping in a posture of disrespect for his feet were turned toward the holy Kaaba, the sacred black stone of the Islamic world. He was rudely awakened and scolded:

"Why have you, O sinner, turned your feet toward God?" Thereupon Nanak retorted: "Turn my feet in the direction in which God is not to be found." He clearly sought to remind the priest of God's omnipresence.

During Nanak's lifetime Babar, the Moghul from Central Asia, invaded India a number of times and in 1526 became the ruler of Delhi. Babar was responsible for much destruction and suffering for he burnt houses, resting places and age-old temples. The invading forces behaved mercilessly. People were tortured ruthlessly. Nanak bewailed:"Has it not awakened any pity in you, O Lord?" These words which seem to reproach God for failing to protect the persecuted are so reminiscent of the last words of the dying Jesus: 'My God, my God, why hast Thou Forsaken me?" There are times when even the holiest of God-men are puzzled by the seemingly irrational and heartless ways of God.

In the evening of his life, Nanak ceased wandering and settled down in the town of Kartapur, where he continued preaching. It was here that his last fifteen years were spent.

Before Nanak died in 1539 at the age of seventy, he selected Guru Angad (1504-1552) to be his spiritual successor for he passed over his own two sons whom he thought unsuitable for the purpose of guiding the fortunes of his nascent religious movement.

The devotional path

Nanak once described himself as a God-intoxicated man who had lost his reason in pursuit of the Lord. He was wholly committed to the path of devotion or Bhakti Marga. Although he was a great devotee himself, he showed the futility of giving expression to that devotion through the performance of austerities and penances because nothing can equal the contemplation of

God's name. Yet in his character there was a streak of asceticism which he sometimes acknowledged. Once in a state of sacrificial piety he declared: "I may cut myself into pieces to gain a glimpse of God."

Throughout the ages the view has prevailed that the experience of God can be bought with the coin of personal suffering. A baby cries in order to draw attention to itself. Is it this very same infantile mentality, which urges so many to engage themselves in physical and psychological self-mortification, and so to immerse themselves in a sea of self-pity, in the hope thereby of obtaining the sympathetic attention of an imagined Supreme Deity?

The nature of the Formless One

Nanak declared:

> "God of Himself created Himself; and He Himself assumed the Name. Second besides Himself, He created Nature wherein He lives and observes it with delight."

The statement that God created himself amounts to saying that God existed prior to his own birth. The statement is as absurd as the claim of a child who says 'I am my own parents!' Had he maintained that God was the First Cause and then pleaded ignorance as to how the Absolute had come into being he would have sounded more convincing. But there is a hymn of his in the *Adi Granth*, which has an unmistakeable Hindu flavour, wherein he contradicts his earlier statement that God had a definite beginning:

> "Pure and without beginning, changeless,
> The same from age to age."

According to Nanak there is but one eternal God, the creator of the universe, who is immortal, unborn and self-existent. When he said that God is the beneficent one who provides sustenance to all living beings and that there is none except God to go to when in need of refuge, this concept of God accords closely with the Judaic-Christian-Islamic notion of the Divine as the great provider and helper, who knows our needs and provides accordingly. But elsewhere in his works his idea of God is more akin to the Hindu view. God is impersonal and formless: "God has neither any form nor material sign."

Is the mind truly capable of imagining something that is formless? Its imaginative powers are inevitably circumscribed by the various images that the mind has retained. Stated differently, it can be said one can imagine only in terms of past rememberings or mental pictures recorded in the brain cells. The imaginative process can operate only because of the existence of these images, all of which have definite forms, shapes and other characteristics. Without the help of these images no imagination is possible. Therefore, is the image-ridden mind capable of thinking about something that is imageless and formless? God, then, is the unthinkable. One can, of course, think about God by reducing him to a mere concept or a word. But can a concept or a word ever accurately represent something which is indescribable?

Nanak remarked that forgetting God even for an instant has to be regarded as a great affliction of the mind. This statement implies that the godly person is one whose mind is constantly fixed on God. Here again it is assumed that God is within the realm of thought. But probably it is the rare individual whose mind is divested of all thought, including the thought of God himself, who discovers God.

God is also omnipresent in the sense that he is all-pervasive. He is everywhere and in all things; nowhere is he not to be found. Nanak picturesquely illustrated this idea: "God Himself is the fish and the fisherman, the water and the net. God is the float of the net as well as the bait within it."

Nanak's conception of God was basically pantheistic in the sense that he identified the Deity with nature. Although God remains unknown, he is still indirectly knowable via nature. God, he asserted, is revealed through nature: "God Himself is invisible but He is always visible through nature."

But how can one understand God through nature when nature's own workings are mysterious enough? Am I being asked to gaze with wonder at the majestic Himalayan mountains and then think of the glory of that self-made abstraction called God? By the same token, must I not also look at the suffering and misery of those who are born blind or crippled and then thank God for having so used nature when giving expression to his creative powers?

According to Nanak, God cannot be understood through cleverness. He taught: "Through God's own grace is God realised." So great a value did he set on the saving grace of God that he insisted that the accumulated effect of past deeds cannot be removed without it. This is a far cry from Buddhism, which upholds that the accumulated effects of past deeds (i.e. Karma) can be eliminated only through one's own efforts: man is his own saviour. Let us now ask a question: what must one do to become eligible to receive God's grace? It is the general view of theists that to qualify for receiving grace one should first of all have achieved a high state of inner purity. The Bible proclaims that the pure in heart are blessed for they shall see God. If purity is the prior condition for receiving God's grace, then must we not revert to the Buddhist position that the state of purity is realizable only by those who single-handedly divest themselves of Karma?

Is destiny determined by karma or God?

We may now turn our attention to the related issue of the law of Karma. Karma is the law of cause and effect. Our misfortunes of today are the consequences of our misdeeds of yesterday. Karma is constituted of psychological memories in the form of unresolved conflicts, hatred jealousy, anger and the like which, not having been cast aside in previous lives, are unfortunately carried over to the present life. Man suffers and is in bondage because he is burdened by the weight of Karma. He is the prisoner of his past Karma and the purgation of his mind of the virus of Karma is Liberation.

That Nanak accepted the doctrine of Karma is obvious from the following two statements of his:

> "We carry with us the record of our deeds."
>
> "One reaps what one sows; one eats what one earns."

Now, if our sorrows were of our own making, would it not be illogical to ascribe them to a power outside ourselves? If the law of Karma were true, then not God, but we alone would be the sole determiners of our destinies. But if the belief in an omnipotent God were true, then he alone would shape the course of our lives. Is it not contradictory to believe, as Nanak evidently did, in God's omnipotence and also to believe in the law of Karma at the same time?

Is God Omnipotent?

Nanak regarded God as the all-powerful supreme being: "Whatever God wills, that occurs; for nothing is in the hands of man." He also stated: "All are yoked to

God's will. and will be judged according to their deeds."

If my will were always overpowered by that of God, even to the extent of reducing me to a status where I would no longer be a free agent, then why should I be held responsible for my deeds? If my will were yoked to that of God, then I would be a mere puppet in the hands of the Almighty. I should rightly be held responsible for my actions, only if I had had a hand in determining them. If God were in total control over man, then should we be blamed for anything 'sinful' that we do? If some persons prefer to turn away from God or even question whether God exists at all, then surely the responsibility for their 'wayward' ways must be fully borne by God himself since man is devoid of freewill ('nothing is in the hands of man')

Nanak often reiterated that the utter powerlessness of man is in direct contradistinction to the omnipotence of God:

> "Whatever happens, is all in Your will."

He affirmed the absolute helplessness of man:

> "You are the doer, O God; I can do nothing.
> Even if I try to do something, I fail."

But the following statement of Nanak makes one question whether the will of God actually supersedes the will of man:

> "He who submits to the will of God, is accepted and treasured by Him."

What is the point of exhorting man to surrender himself to the will of God, unless he were capable of volition himself? So, it is within the power of man to make himself subservient to the will of God! Many theologians, including Nanak himself, failed to realize how confused their thinking was when they, on the one hand, asserted the omnipotence of God's will, and then on the other, rather contradictorily, appealed to man to exercise his own will and thereby accept the overlordship of the Divine. It is necessary to emphasize this point by expressing it differently: If omnipotent God alone exercises will, then ineffectual man is a mere tool in God's hands and hence should be regarded as being blameless for any of his misdeeds; but if man has a limited will which cannot be overridden by the will of God, then why should God be considered as being omnipotent any more?

Why name the Nameless?

Throughout the numerous compositions of Nanak there runs a constant theme — it is by reciting God's name that one discovers him. It is not the learned person who finds God. Neither can he be realized through sacrificial rites nor tedious pilgrimages to so-called sacred shrines in far distant places. But there is hope for the humble devotee who chants the holy name of God:

> "He alone is dear to God who utters his name.'
>
> He sincerely believed the name of God to be the only remedy for the diseased world. Devotion to the name washes away the mind's impurities. Nothing in life is more important:
>
> "Dwell only on God's name; all other deeds are fruitless."
>
> He was never tired of instructing again and again that there can be salvation only via the name of God:
>
> "By repeating God's name, I live; by forgetting it, I die."

Nanak diligently practised what he preached because it was his habit to stop every five minutes whatever he was doing and then close his eyes and say:

"I am Thine, O Lord, I am Thine."

Apparently he had this compulsive urge to be constantly uttering the name of the Lord.

Let us now examine this question of invoking God, which is such an essential and important feature of Nanak's teachings.

First, various saints and seers, including Nanak himself, have asserted that God is ineffable. God is so immeasurably immense that he is beyond the limited description of words. No label, no word, no phrase can do justice to his infinite vastness and splendour. So, by naming God are we not attempting to name the nameless? Why insult God through the media of words of our own making?

Second, *nāma japa* or the repetition of the name of God, a sacred word or phrase is a Hindu religious practice that Nanak conveniently adopted. Through the constant repetition of any word, regardless of whether that word is 'sacred', 'profane', 'obscene' or even meaningless, an artificial state of stillness can certainly be induced. I have seen quite a number of Yogis in India get into trances by this technique. The stream of consciousness or the fluvial thought process gets temporarily halted because of this kind of self-hypnosis and the resultant short-lived quietness is mistakenly called 'bliss'. When the talkative superficial layer of the mind is tranquil, the contents of the unconscious are provided with an opportunity to surface. The hidden layers of the mind then try to communicate with the conscious layer. In this state one experiences 'visions' of God. The various images that the mind had manufactured about God suddenly find expression in the form of 'visions'. The 'God' one sees is nothing more than the mind's own creations — concepts and images of God. The mind can only see what has already been lurking within it. The mind never has a vision that is unrelated to its own existing contents. We see in 'visions' what we have been unconsciously longing to see. Thus the Catholic experiences a 'vision' of the Virgin — he sees his own long-cherished image of Mary. Similarly, the Shaivite saints had 'visions' of Lord Shiva in all his splendour; the Buddhists' 'visions' are confined to the serene Buddha in his saffron-coloured robes. If the Catholic were ever to experience a vision of the Buddha that would be 'miraculous' indeed!

Third, such artificial 'quietening' of the mind is valueless because it is a short-lived experience anyhow. This explains why those who become addicted to this psychological drug have to resort to it again and again. There is a world of difference between a mind that is subdued into a state of spurious stillness on the one hand; and on the other, a mind that suddenly finds itself in a state of natural stillness as a consequence of a deep understanding of its complexities and processes. The former state is induced whereas the latter is like a blessing that comes unsought.

Fourth, God remains the mysterious unknown. Instead of honestly admitting the fact of our total ignorance concerning this matter, we foolishly imagine that we are somehow communicating with 'God' by merely repeating a name that is associated with something that is unknown The name is only a symbol and can never be the actual thing it is supposed to denote. The grandiloquent names that we invent and subsequently worship may not correspond in the least with God. Yet many are committed to the belief that by constantly chanting God's 'name' they are actually experiencing God himself! Nanak did admit that:

> "It is not possible to know your state, O God; but we must express your name, even without knowing it."

If the state of God is not knowable, as Nanak truthfully acknowledged it to be, why not say that the unknowable is ipso facto unnameable?

Fifth, if the repetition of God's name is the condition to be fulfilled whereby man endears himself to God, then must not God be rather vain? Is the Almighty so egoistic that he expects us to sing his praises all the time? Is he going to get hurt and deny us favours merely because we have turned our backs on him? Those who repeat God's name, do so either out of regard for the feelings of God that they dare not ignore, or because such activities are a source of immense self-satisfaction for themselves.

Why Believe in a Soul?

Nanak held the view that everyone is blessed with a soul that is deathless and indestructible. This soul is no other than God himself for God abides in the soul and the soul in God. Something of the Divine inheres in all persons.

The fusion of the individual soul (*ātman*) with the supreme soul (*Paramātman*) or the Divine is a fundamental Hindu belief which was echoed in the following saying of Nanak:

> "If God shows mercy one meditates on Him and one's soul is dissolved and is absorbed in Him. It becomes one with the Supreme Soul and the inner duality disappears."

Let us examine some of the important implications of the belief in the existence of a soul.

First, does it not flatter my vain little ego to think that God is within me?

Second, if God is already part and parcel of my personality, why bother to seek him elsewhere? Indeed, why bother to seek him at all or even worship or praise him because, according to this belief, I am already partly divine?

Third, what am I but a mixture of psychological traits — hurts, prejudices, dislikes, violence, aggression and the like? Now, can God, who is reputedly the purest kind of love, coexist harmoniously with my violence, hatred and other attributes which reveal a lack of love? Is love compatible with hate? We are asking whether characteristics such as these, which are not only mutually contradictory but also mutually exclusive, can ever be found *together* within the same person?

Fourth, if I were really divine in some measure, why did my 'holy' and 'Godly' nature so hopelessly fail to prevent the emergence of these ugly and deplorable non-Godly qualities?

Fifth, within this body is there anything that is changeless and permanent and hence deserving to be designated as the soul? Does the 'soul' really exist in the anatomical sense that the brain exists, or is it a mere figment of the imagination? The term 'soul' is of course an attractive and convenient figurative expression but does it *factually* exist?

Why does the mind create the idea of the 'soul' which is but a synonym for the 'self', the 'ego' or the 'I'? The stream of consciousness is in a state of perpetual flux; it is ever-changing; thoughts, feelings and sensations arise and disappear in rapid succession. The mind develops an antipathy towards this unsettling and uncomfortable state. Hence out of the yearning for permanency in an impermanent situation, the mind craftily creates this concept of the permanent 'soul' or 'self' and then hangs on to it desperately. The self seems real because nearly all our activities are directly or indirectly traceable to the self: seldom do we act selflessly. Still our difficulty is the failure to see that this self which is so central to our psychological world is nothing but a psychological invention. When the self ceases to have an existence of its own, an extraordinary spiritual dimension comes into being. More accurately expressed, the self can never 'cease' because it never tangibly existed in the first place; what ceases is not the self but the illusion of the self. Despite his aforementioned belief in a soul, Nanak himself had a remarkable insight into this mystery:

> "Where the self exists,
> God is not;
> Where God exists,
> The self is not."

Why Restrain the Wayward Mind?

Nanak complained that the mind is as wayward as a drunken elephant. He admonished: "Restrain the unsteady mind and keep it in its place." Is the nature of the entity that is trying to restrain the mind any different from the nature of the mind itself? That entity, the ego, the 'I', which tries to control and discipline the mind is a product of the mind itself and hence it inescapably bears all the traits of the mind. If the mind is 'wayward' then the ego will also be similarly 'wayward': it cannot be otherwise since the 'I' is of the same substance as the mind wherefrom it originated.

For example, what actually happens if any attempt were made to restrain anger? Is not the agency that tries to squash anger also a part of the angry mind? That agency or the 'I' was conceived and nurtured in an environment of anger. So with an assumed air of moral superiority, the 'I' which is itself seething with anger, tries vainly to subjugate anger as though anger were something external to itself! Thus when anger confronts anger in open conflict, what is there but increased anger? All talk of restraint arises from failing to comprehend the basic truth that the dualistic approach to psychological problems is hardly the solution. When the mind is 'unsteady' any attempt to tame it will only result in making it unsteadier and more boisterous. But if one cares to observe the mind gently, just watch all its various movements without interfering with it in any way whatsoever, it will be found that the mind unfolds itself and becomes quiet and orderly.

Why be Guided by Gurus?

The idea of *guruship* is cardinal aspect of Sikh doctrine. The very word 'Sikh' means *sishya* or disciple and the Sikhs are a community of disciples who believe in their ten Gurus.

Nanak is reported to have told a Muslim: "At God's gate there is no room for a prophet." If this statement were meant to be taken literally and seriously, then one should view with an element of scepticism the doings and sayings of all intermediaries between God and man, such as prophets and Gurus. Yet in the *Adi Granth* he stated:

> "The word of the Guru is the highest scripture;
> The word of the Guru is all-pervading."

He went to the extent of identifying the Guru with God:

> "The Guru is God, ineffable, unsearchable. He who follows the Guru understands the nature of the universe."

Is it possible to realize God without the assistance and directions of a Guru? Apparently he regarded the role of the Guru as indispensable for God realization:

> "God is made known to men by the grace of the Guru, the enlightener."

He also declared:

"No person has realised God without the grace of the true Guru."

In view of these pronouncements, let us probe a bit further. If God is not discoverable without the help of a Guru, then how did the very first person in history who succeeded in realizing God, whoever that unknown person might have been, manage to do so? That very first person who drank the waters of the Divine could not have had a predecessor as a guide precisely because he was the *first*; he was a pioneer in that field and he must have explored entirely uncharted waters. Besides, as there are so many Gurus who propound conflicting theories and beliefs, have I the clarity of mind to tell the genuine Guru from the false? For I can only pick and choose a spiritual teacher only in accordance with the particular manner in which my mind has been conditioned with its many beliefs, ideas, aversions, predilections and a thousand other unknown factors that continually distort my perception. This means that because I am confused and in the dark myself, do I really have the intelligence to select the right Guru in such a state of mind? And if I happen to have that intelligence, then will I ever need a Guru?

Many persons are guided by their intuition in this matter of selecting a suitable Guru. But, what is the point of relying on intuition which is itself the product of psychological conditioning? Flashes of 'intuition' and 'Divine inspiration' are particularly untrustworthy because they do not emanate from outside the field of conditioned consciousness but from within it.

Nanak had an unshakeable faith in the efficacy of Gurus! One wishes he had foreseen how his own teachings were subjected to alteration at the hands of subsequent Gurus and interpreters. As we shall see later in this chapter, the gentle character which pervaded the teachings of Nanak was considerably changed by one of his successors, Guru Gobind Singh, who introduced into them an element of militarism.

Nanak Preached Social Equality

Egalitarian sentiments pervaded Nanak's religious movement for he denounced caste and class distinctions and sought to establish a community open to all. He tried hard to excise the cancer of the age-old caste system that separated otherwise friendly people.

Nanak was forthright in his denunciation of the evils inherent in this system. Had his utterances been taken seriously he would probably have succeeded in radically altering the structure of Indian society. According to him the truly religious person considers all as equals. God, he observed, does not mind our caste for it is "One's deeds which proclaim one's caste."

A man will be judged not by his ancestry but his behaviour. When Nanak condemned the caste system he was not being particularly original because several centuries earlier Gautama, the Buddha, too, had strongly spoken against it and indicated that one becomes a Brahmin not by virtue of birth but by leading a life of inner purity. In the *Dhammapada* the Buddha eloquently described the hallmarks of a true Brahmin and one of these is worthy of consideration: "The man who is free from possessions and desires — him I call a Brahmin." The Buddha's reasons for opposing the caste system were somewhat different from those of Nanak. According to the Buddha, the true Brahmin is free from desires. Presumably, then, a genuinely pure person would be free even from the desire to realize God.

In the eyes of the Almighty there are no higher or lower degrees of human beings. Nanak believed that God's benediction descended only when the lowly were looked after. Probably because he wanted others to emulate him, Nanak said that he sought the company of the lowest of the low-born.

If one is moved to decry the caste system, as indeed one should be, then let not any criticisms of it originate from a mere theological dogma about God to which one happens to be emotionally attached, but rather let it spring from a sincere concern for the welfare of those sections of society who have long been suppressed and downtrodden.

The original lofty theory of a religion is often far removed from its actual practice. It is indeed disappointing that caste distinctions are not unknown among modern Sikhs. They are composed of many tribes and castes. It has been estimated that nearly half the Punjab Sikhs are Jat Sikhs, a caste group.

Questionable Hindu practices

Nanak was unsparing in his criticism of certain Hindu religious practices. He said that the mind cannot be purified by worshipping stones, visiting holy places, living in forests and wandering about as ascetics. He likened rituals and ceremonies to the chains of the mind. But the singing of God's praise was for him like a pilgrimage to Benares and bathing in the Ganga. He also disapproved of the practice of visiting tombs and crematoria. What really mattered in life was not the dissipation of one's precious energies and time in useless pursuits but rather the worship of the one God. His unwavering monotheism had a pronounced Islamic flavour:

> "God, the one alone, is everywhere. Since there is no one like God, to whom else are we to make an offering in worship?"

He was indirectly attacking those Hindus who believed in many gods instead of worshipping the one and only God. Still he was sufficiently imbued with Hindu thought to maintain that true Yoga consists in dwelling in God, and remaining detached while surrounded by worldly attachments.

Some writers have stated that Nanak blended Hinduism with Islam. Is such a statement correct? Blending is the action of mixing together different elements so that their original distinguishing features are no longer discernible. He did not blend the two religions in this sense, because his various ideas and beliefs are easily traceable to their two main sources. It would be more correct to say that he borrowed some of the doctrines of Hinduism and Islam and combined them, thereby creating his own distinct religious system. In a subtle way he rejected both religious traditions but at the same time accepted certain doctrines in them that he deemed appropriate. It is an interesting fact that he preferred to write his hymns in Gurmukhi instead of the Sanskrit of the Hindus or the Arabic of the Muslims.

Sect of the Purified

The Sikhs suffered religious persecution under the imperial Mughal rulers and they reacted to the violence of their oppressors by becoming militarily assertive and violent themselves. The ninth Guru, Tegh Bahadur, was beheaded at Delhi in 1675. His son, Guru Gobind Singh (1666-1708), the tenth and last Guru, fought the Moghals as well as the neighbouring Hindu rajas. Gobind Singh's two elder sons were killed in battle and his remaining two younger sons were captured and done to death by the order of the Muslim Subedar of Sirhind. Gobind Singh's own life came to a tragic end in 1708 when he was fatally stabbed by two Pathans who were sent by the Subedar to kill him.

In 1699 Gobind Singh was responsible for instituting

the Khālsā-Panth ('Sect of the Purified' which is derived from the Persian *khalis*, 'the pure'). He wanted the Sikhs to be soldiers and he instilled them with militaristic values in order to help them defend their faith against the Mughals. Let us recall the famous lines of this Guru:

"When all other resources fail
Resorting to the sword is legitimate."

Through the instrumentality of the *khālsā* he wanted to transform the Sikhs into a militant fraternity. This concept of a brotherhood of believers is rather Islamic. The establishment of Khālsā is a landmark in the history of Sikhism.

Before a vast assembly of Sikhs, Gobind Singh announced that he wanted the heads of five persons. Thereupon five men offered themselves to be sacrificed. He took them behind a tent and returned with his blood-smeared sword. But he had slain five goats instead of the men. The persons who offered themselves for sacrifice became the first members of the new order. They are mentioned in the Sikh daily prayer as *panj pyare*, the five beloved ones of the Guru.

Along with these five, thousands more joined the *khālsā*. They were all ceremonially initiated into the order. The initiates were administered with *amrit* (sweetened water in an iron bowl which was ritually stirred with a dagger and sanctified by the recitation of the scripture). The purpose of this ceremony was to ensure that the participants committed their lives to the Guru's ideals.

In accordance with the spirit of brotherhood, henceforth no caste distinctions would be observed. So that caste names could be done away with, all males were to use the surname 'Singh', and similarly all females were to use the surname *'Kaur'*.

Moral values, heroism and discipline were highly emphasised in the sect. When a Sikh is initiated (*pahul*), he undertakes the observance of certain vows and obligations. Some of the more important of these are noteworthy. He repudiates all ideas of caste and polytheistic deities (this amounts to a rejection of popular Hinduism); he promises to abstain from the four *kurahāts* (misdeeds): the shaving or cutting of his hair or beard, eating meat killed in the traditional manner practised by the Muslims, adultery and the use of intoxicants or tobacco. Those who engage themselves in a *kurahāt* become apostates. After performing penance for their misconduct they have to receive fresh initiation. Furthermore, he undertakes to observe five vows (the "five K's") which were, and still are, the outward marks for identifying a Sikh: *kesh* — to wear their hair and beards unshorn as a symbol of the saintly devotee, *kara* — to wear a steel bracelet on their right wrist as a symbol of self-control in action, *kachh* — to wear shorts or drawers as a symbol of activity in service, *Kangh* — to carry a comb as a symbol of discipline and order and *kirpan* — to carry a dagger or sword as a symbol of courage and self-respect.

The belief prevails that by joining the *khālsā* one becomes a part of the Guru's own body through whom the Guru carries out his mission in the world; one becomes a member of a distinct religious group with a heroic tradition. It is normal for *khālsā* organizations to argue that only the Khālsā Sikhs are the genuine Sikhs. But there are the dissident Sahaj-Dhāri Sikhs who claim to adhere to the original teachings of Nanak and the earlier Gurus before the advent of Gobind Singh. There are also the Nanakpanthi (also known as Nanakshāhi) who disagree with the teachings of Gobind Singh for they prefer to follow the peaceful and devotional path to God as taught by Nanak.

Throughout history have not religious differences and national loyalties, let alone social, caste and racial distinctions, been the curse of mankind? Have not all such divisions resulted in alienating people? Instead of having one united family of human beings, we are faced with a bewildering mass of warring factions, each of which egoistically asserts its own interests and supposed superiority. A proud cloud may regard itself as being separate from the sky but it still remains a part of the immense firmament; a haughty wave may consider itself as an independent entity when in fact it is only a part of the vast ocean. Similarly, groups of people seek for themselves a status of isolated exclusiveness, forgetting the truth that they belong to the one ocean of humanity. The *khālsā* ostensibly abolished caste but because it inculcated a new self-consciousness upon the Sikh community, it virtually created a new caste in an already caste-ridden Indian society. Insofar as the institution of the *khālsā* resulted in isolating the Sikhs from the rest of mankind, did it really promote brotherhood? Of what value is the 'brotherhood' that supposedly exists within a community, if that community's relationship with the outside world is subject to discord, suspicion or hostility? Any kind of clannishness, even when it is based on 'spirituality', inevitably results in injuring the pride and hurting the feelings of those who do not belong to the sect that promotes it. So the founding of the *khālsā* may be viewed as a retrogressive step, especially because the spirit of true religion consists in the total elimination of *all* barriers and the consequent fostering of a genuine brotherhood and unity of man.

Finally, as mentioned before, Sikhism has its own authoritative scripture, the *Granth* or the *Adi Granth*, which is also reverently referred to as *Granth Sahib* or

Guru Granth Sahib. This book is treated as the living Guru, particularly because of the statement of Gobind Singh that the *Granth* would henceforth be regarded as the Guru and that there would be no more Gurus. With the abolishing of personal *guruship*, this work became the ultimate authority on all doctrinal and other questions. Since the *Granth* is the holy scripture through the medium of which the Guru talks to his devotees it is often called the *Guru Granth* or *Gurbani* (the Guru's voice). Because of the belief that the light of Guru Nanak's soul was transmitted to all his nine successors in turn, the Sikhs regard the ten Gurus as only *one* person in the spiritual sense. Hence it is maintained that the *Granth* is the verbal expression of that one Guru.

The *Granth*, which is also widely accepted as the greatest work in Punjabi literature, owes its existence to the efforts of its compiler, Guru Arjan (1563-1606), the fifth Guru. This book contains the works of some forty-two poet-saints. It may be likened therefore to the Bible, which is also a compilation of the writings of many different authors who lived at different periods. So the reader of books of such variegated authorship should not be surprised to find therein the existence of contradictions of various kinds.

The *Granth* may be described as a fine anthology of devotional outpourings that have been taken from the Hindu and Muslim religious traditions of India — traditions that had often been in conflict.

It is necessary to distinguish between the *Granth* and the *Dasam Granth*, which is a compilation of over 2,000 hymns by Gobind Singh. Whereas nearly all Sikhs accept the authority of the *Granth*, this is not the case with the *Dasam Granth* which is acceptable only to certain sections.

There are no graven images of God nor any deities in Gurudwārās (Sikh temples) in accordance with Nanak's condemnation of idolatry:

"He cannot be placed like an idol
Nor can man shape His likeness."

How can any image, symbol or picture, however beautiful it may happen to be, ever truly represent the infinite limitlessness of the Absolute? Nanak was probably influenced by Islamic teaching which rejects all forms of idolatry.

In theory there is no idolatry in Sikhism, but in practice the *Granth* has become a sort of idol. Those entering a place where the *Granth* is enshrined should have just bathed, wear clean clothes and cover their heads. They deferentially bow to it before sitting in its presence.

In the Golden Temple at Amritsar, the sanctum sanctorum of the Sikh world, the *Granth* is venerated as deity. In the mornings it is dressed in brocade and placed on a throne under the canopy adorned with jewels. Then at night the book rests on a golden bed.

At Amritsar Gurudwara, the *Granth* is the only religious object to be found, and relays of priests take turns to read it continuously every day. It is claimed that it has been read uninterruptedly ever since 1577. When it is being read a fly-whisk is constantly waved over it in slow graceful movements.

Also the names chosen for the Sikhs depend on this holy book. A selected name has to begin with the initial of the first word on the page that is found when the *Granth* is opened at random.

And at Sikh weddings no Brahmin priest officiates; no Vedic texts are recited nor is there any colourful sacred fire. But the *Granth* is circumambulated instead of the fire and the union sanctified by reciting extracts from it.

SELECT BIBLIOGRAPHY

CHETHIMATTAM, John B. *Patterns of Indian thought*. London: Geoffrey Chapman, 1971 *Encyclopaedia of Religion and Ethics*; edited by James Hastings. Edinburgh: T. & T. Clark, 1959

Encyclopaedia of Religion and Ethics; edited by James Hastings. Edinburgh: T. & T. Clark, 1959

GREENLEES, Duncan. *The Gospel of the Guru-Granth Sahib. Madras: Theosophical Publishing House, 1975*

Kushwant Singh's View of India; edited by Rahul Singh. Bombay: IBH Publishing Company, 1982

McLEOD, Hew. Sikhism (In A *Cultural History of India*; edited by A.L. Basham. Delhi: Oxford University Press, 1983).

POTTER, C.F. *The Great Religious Leaders*. New York: Simon and Schuster. 1958

Religions of India. New Delhi: Clarion Books, 1983

Sayings of Guru Nanak. (An anthology compiled by Harnam Singh Shan). Amritsar: Dharam Parchar Committee, S.G.P.C., circa 1969)

Selections from the Sacred Writings of the Sikhs. London: George Allen & Unwin, 1965

SPIEGELBERG, Frederic. *Living Religions of the World. London: Thames and Hudson, 1957*